The Siachen Soldier
and other stories

The Siachen Soldier
and other stories

Air Cmde Nitin Sathe
Poetry by Suneet Madan

Vitasta

Published by
Renu Kaul Verma
Vitasta Publishing Pvt Ltd
4348/4C, Ansari Road, Daryaganj
New Delhi-110 002
info@vitastapublishing.com

ISBN: 978-81-19670-98-7
© Prose Nitin Sathe
© Poems Suneet Madan
First Edition 2024
MRP ₹350

All Rights Reserved.
No part of this publication may be reproduced, stored in a retrieval system, or transmitted in any form, or by any means – electronic, mechanical, photocopying, recording or otherwise – without the prior permission of the publisher.

Edited by Ankita Athawale and Alisha Verma
Typeset & Cover Design by Somesh Kumar Mishra
Printed by Vikas Computer and Printers, New Delhi

Contents

Preface	*vii*
A Happy Pause	1
A Home on Wheels	7
Staying in Touch	18
Into the 'Deep'	22
Surviving the Seniors	28
The Siachen Soldier	34
Proud Flier	43
The Metal Bird	48
My Cockpit My Home	53
Landing Happy	60
The 'Hood'	66

Perspective in Flying	70
Fueling Man and Machine	75
The Customary Cheers!	83
The Queen Comes Calling	90
Man Friday	98
Home Away From Home	106
Pottering on A Train	114
Uff…Will She, Won't She?	120
'Lost' Stories	128
Cats Have Nine Lives And Pilots?	135
Dust to Dust	142
Unforgiving Omission	146
Gestures of Gratitude	152
Kick That Tyre and Light The Fire…	159
Zest For Life	162
Detailed to Kill	168
Waves That Changed Lives	176
Other Books By The Author	*181*

Preface

'Hey, I have an idea! Let's put my short stories and your poems together in a book.' This idea from Nitin was the genesis of this medley of Poetry and Prose which led to the neologistic creation of "Poestries" by Suneet.

While Nitin spins true stories out of the rotors of his helicopter, based on his experiences in the Indian Air Force, Suneet knits her magical words around the central theme of each story to make this book a unique, mindful and interesting read. *Jugalbandi* of sorts, with each on its own course of discovery.

Having created poetry or prose through the night, writers most often don't quite admire their own work when day breaks. Imagine the scene with two writers, both writing in their unique and different styles, pulling in different directions, coming on common ground to agree. And thus, this jointly written introduction, written in both first and third person, will sound tangential and divergent. Abstract? Vague? We both thought so too. But then, once you go through the amalgam of poetry and prose this book offers you–the reader–you would understand what we mean.

This book has been written while the world was going through extremely troubled times. Come to think of it, living and surviving in those times whilst keeping your sanity intact has all been a game of the mind. What we think of as hardship and where we draw the line of our forbearance–it begins and ends right there, in the head.

In recounting his years in the Indian Air Force, Nitin was struck by the fact that all the trials and hardships, as also the fun, frolic and glory–all those moments that seemed so important at one time–were now only the stuff for stories. And therefore, the troubles of today will become seeds for the stories of the morrow.

As we put this book out into the world, we pray for safety and hope that these easy-to-read stories and poems serve as motivation or inspiration in those moments when you think all isn't well with life.

As they say in the Air Force, we wish you happy landings and blue skies!

Before you start out to read, we express our deep gratitude to Renu Kaul Verma, our friend and publisher at Vitasta Publications. Thank you Renu for bestowing your trust in us, and being equally enthusiastic in bringing out this *jugalbandi* for you.

We would also like to thank our families and friends who helped in many ways to shape up this book. Sincere thanks to the men and women who come to life in this book, and, last but not least, to you, the booklover. The written world is incomplete until it finds a reader.

You got the controls now... Read on!

We'd love to hear your comments on

poestries@gmail.com

A Happy Pause

.... ❖ ....

Trying to pick up pace in the wild goose chase
I feel lost and dazed in the compounding maze
Growing more alien by the day to my own face
Despite being at home, completely out of place

In the fleeting look the reflection looks unclear
Who I was seeking in the mirror, did not appear
Hidden in the forest of emotions like a shy deer
Paucity of time did not let me go anywhere near

In the haste to achieve everything at the earliest
I failed to acknowledge what was truly the best
Aiming to make the elusive carrot my conquest
Missing out crucial essentials in the futile quest

God is in the details but I ignored the implication
Neglecting the journeys in search of destination
Lamenting the lacks than praising the possessions
Until I realised the value of pausing for reflection

She leans across the seat suddenly and peers at the slick instrument panel of our SUV. 'What do you think you are doing?' I ask, distracted by the glossy white road markers disappearing into the black tarmac below me.

This drive along the white centre line of the road has taken me back to my days of flying. I imagine myself on take-off roll in my small jet on which I learnt to fly. I miss it all now. How I wish I could rewind to my younger days again!

'Don't be so touchy! I just want to know the speed we are travelling at!' she snaps, sounding more irritated than I am.

'Duh-uh—120 kilometres per hour', my equally sour reply stops further conversation. She returns to her mobile and I return to my reverie back in time.

The highways are nice and broad, smooth as silk with no distracting traffic. Of course, there is the occasional loony car or truck trying to outrun an SUV or some cattle or carts slowing you down once a while. But dreaming is easy on these roads.

It is 1972, I am an eight-year-old travelling with family in our 1963 model 'Amby'. I still remember her registration–MRZ-6738. She is third-hand and old.

With a new coat of paint with every new owner, she belies her age. A few dents here and there and a small gash add character to her contours. Other than that, she could as well pass off for new!

Her well-tuned engine purrs like a cat, guzzling a litre of petrol to propel us 8 kms. Petrol, incidentally, is 65 paise to a litre and news is that it will cross a rupee soon! My dad fills me up with technical trivia as he guns the engine to accelerate to 50-60 miles per hour on this wide-open Grand Trunk road. 'That means we are going almost 80-90 kmph...' he says with a smile and running his big burly hands through my oily hair, explains how to convert MPH to KMPH.

'That is really fast!' I exclaim, my eyes sparkling with ever growing admiration for my father. I have never seen the odometer cross 30 before. The odometer in our car reads 'miles-per-hour', when it works.

As my father explains the colour coding on the milestones and the markings on the bridges and culverts, the car swerves suddenly and the conversation stops. There is a whoosh and hiss indicating we have a blowout. Dad, as usual, shows what a cool cucumber he is. He swiftly manoeuvres us to the edge of the road and brings us to a halt, cursing under his breath.

'Puncture!' he announces with a smile to my terrified mother, who is still clutching me to her bosom. 'Just 5 minutes,' he says waving his five fingers like a fan at us. He opens the boot and we help him offload the suitcases and knick-knacks to make way for the spare wheel.

I watch Daddy and wonder how and when I will become multi-talented as him. What a hero. One day, perhaps, I will change the tyre for him.

My father grunts under his breath as he pulls the tyre out of the car.

'Ohh... Tragedy! This one too, is deflated!' he pronounces.

Mother now lets him have a mouthful, 'You are travelling with kids, you haven't even checked the car to see if it is fit for the drive. How are we going to get to Delhi?' The tirade continues whilst dad considers the future course of action.

There is a small village close by, a few hundred meters from the main road where we stand looking for help. As a god sent, a bullock-cart appears on the dirt track which connects the village to the highway. The man on the cart sports a bright turban and a long grey beard. He beckons to Daddy with his big round eyes.

In a blink of an eye, we see Daddy sitting alongside the man, with the two wheels of our car thrown carelessly at the back of the cart. The helpful stranger is taking dad to a nearby puncture repair shop.

It is quite a funny sight! Till now, the only vehicle other than this car that I have seen dad in is his snazzy jeep, in which he always sits in front, his smart starched dress punctuated with bright ribbons and stars, driven by an equally smart driver.

While we wait, some ladies come walking by with their children in tow, and seeing us standing in the sun, offer help. A child is sent back to the village to organise a *Khaat* for us to sit on. A few girls bring a couple of brass jugs of cool water and *chaanch*; surely a blessing in this heat.

We are so happy and lucky to be looked after by these angels of mercy and thank them profusely.

'*Arre*!... this is nothing!' they tell us, 'We need to thank you (meaning Daddy, obviously) all the more for being the brave soldiers you are; guarding our borders and helping us live in peace!' says the senior lady in Punjabi interspersed with broken Hindi. My eyes sparkle and my ears turn bright and warm with pride. They can make out that we are a *fauji* family!

I smile thinking of the 'good ol' times', coming back to the road and the present.

We travel these days at almost double speeds, on tubeless tyres which seldom deflate, in air-conditioned and noiseless environments, having no time for anything but the GPS, music and the mobile.

Going purely by the laws of Physics, traveling at a higher speed would mean that we would see more of the world in the same time available.

Does this theory not work in life? I wonder, as I compare the speed of the helicopter I fly with that of the airplane. Choppers fly low and slow and one is able to appreciate the sights from above better than one would in a fast-moving jet.

When we travel fast in life, we miss seeing the village folk, the bullock carts, the smell of the grass mixed with dung, the *khaat* and the *chaanch* served in brass tumblers and of course the lush green views so refreshing to the eyes.

Perhaps, one needs a puncture to slow us down now and then.

A Home On Wheels

.... ❖ ....

Graffiti - a fusion of thoughts and feelings
Subconscious aflame with experiences appealing
Reshaping realisations with passing time
Making such evolutions special and sublime

Reminiscing the numerous journeys and explorations
Picking memories from the mind's oceans
Time heals or do we tend to slowly forget
Moments that impacted us, while cherishing the rest

This is the story of a special journey in a special train that I haven't forgotten for 50 years.

It is 1972. I am an eight-year-old boy. Daddy has just come back from the war and he is going to be the Commanding Officer of a new unit at Hyderabad. Every day, some shiny new equipment or the other lands up by train. Sometimes, there are big Russian guns newly acquired by the army and sometimes new jeeps and trucks; and along with them come officers and men posted in to make up the new 'formation'.

I get a chance to go to the railway station to see the offloading and ask Daddy if I can hitch a ride in those huge monster trucks, that are used to tow the big guns, being offloaded. Dad is kind and I am thrilled.

Over a few weeks, almost all equipments have arrived and the unit commences training to become war-worthy. After all, the unit needs to get used to the new equipments to form a well-knit team of men and machines capable of launching artillery shells accurately at the enemy when required. After about three months of rigorous training, orders are received to move the unit to a place called Nabha in Punjab, so that the unit will be ready to be deployed on the western border at short notice.

There is excitement all around. I wonder how all the eighteen big guns with their allied equipments and men are going to travel this long journey from Hyderabad to the Western border. I approach my father, 'Daddy, how will the unit go to Nabha?'

'Will the Kraz trucks pull the guns all the way to that place?' An idea is taking shape in my head. Perhaps dad may allow me to go from Hyderabad to Nabha on these trucks? No harm dreaming *na*? One always lives in hope!

He smiles and threading his big fingers through my hair replies, 'We are going there in a ***special*** train!'

I am all ears now.

'What is a special train? Will we also get to travel on the train? How much time will it take? How will we have our food and will we be able to take our Jimmy along?' Jimmy is our pet dog and a member of our family.

I have so many questions for Daddy. He listens to me and in reply, simply smiles and starts answering them one by one.

'A special train will take all of us together from here and it will take almost a week to reach our destination. You will soon see how we will go…' he is interrupted by the telephone which keeps him busy over the next few days. I don't trouble him anymore and spend my days dreaming about the journey that is yet to happen.

Over the next few days, the entire unit is packed and there is hustle and bustle all around the campus. I realise what a lot of planning and hard work goes into a move as big as this one. On a weekend, Daddy takes me to the railway siding where a few wagons have arrived. Each of them has to be shunted by a small diesel engine to a ramp so that the vehicles and guns can be driven on to the flat top wagons. It is a slow and tedious process but interesting to watch for a budding young soldier like me. I see for myself how the tracks are switched and how the wagons are shackled to the engine. I also managed to get a ride in one, an amazing experience.

I narrate all this to my friends in school and they are quite envious of me. Not all boys are as lucky as me to get a ride in a real railway engine.

One Sunday, my friends and I go to the railway yard for a 'picnic'. Our mummies have packed our tiffins with goodies which we shall soon share and enjoy. We sit near the abandoned tracks and watch the buzzing activity with great interest. Commotion near the loading area attracts our attention. The wheel of one of the big Russian guns has slipped from the side of the wagon. The gun now hangs precariously and threatens to topple onto the tracks. Everyone rushes to help. A crane is quickly brought at the site to set things right.

Perhaps, this is my first lesson in emergency management and teamwork.

The serpentine train keeps growing by the day and we now await the passenger bogies which will be our homes for the long journey. In a few days, a few first and second class carriages get attached to the middle of the train and all seems to be set. As I follow Daddy for the final inspection of the train, I observe that there are marked box cars for the cook house, office, arms and ammunition and even the Medical Inspection Room. What is most intriguing is, that there is a wagon dedicated to the Unit *Mandir* or *sarva-dharma-sthal*, where prayers for all religions may be offered.

Dad tells me that some of the soldiers will be living inside the big trucks to guard the guns and equipments on the flat bed trailers. Jokingly, he tells me, 'If you create mischief, you too will be travelling inside one of those trucks! So better behave during the journey!' Not an unexciting prospect. A day long detention in one of those trucks may well be exciting. Of course, I can't say that to my father.

It is D Day and we depart with a lot of fanfare. Our bogies are overflowing with flowers, coloured ribbons and balloons tied to the windows of the bogies. There has been a Pooja and even the trucks and guns are decked with orange marigolds. A band plays some melodious marching tunes and lots of people from the cantonment have come to see us off.

One very senior uncle, who even my dad salutes, is there to flag us off. The whistles blow from all corners of the station indicating 'all set' to my dad who takes permission from uncle to get the train moving. They both shake hands and my dad gets a pat on his back as he salutes uncle. A large green flag is then handed over to uncle who waves it ceremoniously. The train slowly chugs out of the platform. The rattle and jingle of the wheels is music to my ears!

We have compartments in the first-class cabin. They have names on the doors and there is a telephone in each cabin as well as on each wagon. Daddy says that it is good to remain in touch with everyone whilst on the move for better 'Command and Control'. I nod my head as if I understand. I think it means Daddy or his other officers can speak to the train driver or guard whenever they need to, and maybe, order them to start or stop the train!

The women go about setting up the cabins for the long journey; bedrolls are opened, pillows inflated and there is even a clothesline inside the compartment. We go from cabin to cabin getting our pets together. Jimmy seems to be enjoying the ride already. The pets yelping and barking and the kids shouting and screaming makes everyone forget the rattle and rumble of the wheels for a while.

My friends and I continue on our exploratory adventure. We discover a coupe with a small bar. The uncle there treats us to some chips and a fizzy drink each. There are crates of beer and some other bottles lined up in a corner which is for our dads. We find another cabin set up as a card room with a table covered with a white cloth in between the bunks and a lot of pillows strewn around. The older lot will soon be here, playing Rummy and Bridge. We are rather pleased with this discovery because it means we will be able to carry on with our adventures and explorations while our parents are glued to their cards for a while.

The train passes through green fields with crops swaying in the breeze. At one station, I jump on to the platform with Jimmy for a quick look around. By the time I return to our bogie, tables have been laid, music is playing on the record player, and hot piping lunch is being served in style. On the platform this train stops anytime, anywhere and for as much time as Daddy orders.

We are off again after lunch. Evening comes and life on the train continues in the gentle swaying and the din. It all feels like a party on the go. The bar warms up to uncles having their drinks in the corridor and discussing all kinds of topics. The war has just ended and everyone has a story to tell. How I wish I was a bit older then… all those tales would have ended up in my book. The evening fun extends late into the night.

It's been a fascinating and happy first day in this special train, our new home. Tomorrow morning, we shall be arriving at a big town where we expect a warm welcome. I am looking forward to seeing some friends who were in school with me but left when their fathers went away on posting.

The tired families retire for the night into their cabins for a well-deserved rest. Come morning, all of us are woken up by stillness and silence, and this, coupled with the reduced hum of the of the fans, indicate that we have arrived. The sky is lighting up on the eastern horizon and the birds are stretching their wings to get ready for their day. We are reluctant to leave our bunks and need to be cajoled to wake up with a promise of a good time.

Lots of people are at the station to receive us–uncles and aunties and some children too. Our train is parked in one corner of the big station and the area has been sealed off by tents and barricades. We have a longish halt here for breakfast. There are several water bowsers and some 'field' toilets which have been parked just outside the platform so that we can freshen up. Mother insists that we bathe in better conditions and wear some fresh clothes and look good for our hosts.

We are soon treated to a sumptuous breakfast of *dosa, idli* and *wada* at a stall set up only for us. The breakfast ends with hot *jalebis,* coffee and juice for us. I get to play with my old friends for a while and then we are off again.

I pray for this ride to go on forever. And it does. Well, almost.

There is never a dull moment on this journey. Our country is so vast and the landscape changes every few hours. We are passing by so many places on my atlas. I have fun marking each one and identifying the route of the train on my book of maps.

One afternoon, the aunties take over the kitchen and the cooking staff is happy for this rest. We are in awe of these ladies who have lined up a feast of *puri, halwa* and *chana* despite the difficult working conditions they must have encountered. We can't thank our mothers enough for this treat and Daddy promises a special something for the ladies in return when we arrive at Delhi the next day. Most of us children have not been to the capital city and look forward to seeing skyscrapers, broad roads, traffic and all the glitter that the city has to offer.

As we reach the outskirts of Delhi, I am quite disappointed to see many poor people living in pitiable conditions along the railway tracks and the rubbish strewn all around. The train is moving agonisingly slow and keeps stopping every few minutes. I am getting impatient. Daddy explains that we need to give way to the other mail and express trains which have higher priority. I overhear him telling someone that the railway authorities are yet undecided where we are to park for the night. Another uncle gives us a talk on how we need to be environment friendly and how disciplined we need to be about managing our waste. He asks us to write an essay on the topic, and we do so enthusiastically in the time that it takes to reach the station.

'The best one will get a bottle of *Cola*,' my Dad motivates us. We know, that in the end, we all will get one!

The train finally creaks to a halt on an old dilapidated platform in a dark corner of Old Delhi railway station.

The area is cordoned off to keep curious onlookers at bay. There are guards with their weapons all around the train too and it looks like a scene from a movie.

So far, it has been a good expedition barring a few hiccups. A few men got left behind as they went searching for some vegetables in a field, someone's little something falling off the running train and one poor goat becoming meat; all this and some technical issues that we only got a whiff of. Wireless sets have been sending daily progress reports to HQ. The office work has been continuing as per routine too. Dad speaks to his men and tells them to be extra careful and not saunter away into the night. He doesn't want any mishap or incident, neither any headlines in the newspapers of the national capital.

The dingy platform is cleaned up and lit. With red *durries* on the floor along with tables, chairs and light music, the dark and dingy place is transformed. Dinner is served and the platform party is wrapped up early. We do not want to make a nuisance in the city and that too on a railway platform. Dad has something up his sleeve anyway. He has requisitioned a few cars, thanks to his connections in the capital. The next day, barring a few officers and men who stay with the train, all of us are taken for a ride through the city and we look forward to watching a movie at a theatre in the evening. There is a cinema hall in Connaught Place where Daddy has booked tickets for the newly released *Seeta aur Geeta*. We, the kids thoroughly enjoy the antics of Hema Malini in a dual role and are in splits throughout the movie.

This is also the first time I have been to a late night show. The promised *Cola* and popcorn make the movie even more worthwhile, thanks to my clever dad.

After the movie, we all go to India Gate. The lawns and the sights of the Rashtrapati Bhavan and Parliament House in the background with *Kwality* ice-cream in the middle of the night has never been forgotten.

And then, best of all, we get to return to our bunks on the train and our life on wheels. Sometime during the night, the train gets on with the journey.

As we enter Punjab, there are miles and miles of fields. The crops are turning a light yellow from green. 'The granary of the nation,' I hear many people say. Later that night, we are treated to an amazing sight of fireflies lighting up among trees in pitch darkness.

'We should be at Nabha in a few hours,' Daddy announces the next morning. Winding up and packing commences to get ready to leave our train-home.

The quaint little town of Nabha, awaits the new unit. A welcome party is set to receive us, with the band and fanfare, of course. Nabha is going to be our new home for the next two years at least. New school, new friends, new adventures.

I am sad that the journey is over. I feel the rolling and swaying motion of the train and miss the rattle and tattle of the wheels for many days after we leave the train. I guess I am lucky to have had an experience of such a special journey on such a special train.

It has been years since this happened. Trains have continued to intrigue me more than planes. Thanks to being a part of our armed forces and travelling all over our nation's tracks, I have been privileged to have had many interesting journeys which I have recounted in my travelogues. But this journey in the special train from Hyderabad to Nabha will continue to hold a special place in my heart.

Staying In Touch

.... ❖ ....

Words delivering health and infirmities of mind
Recording the context and content of lexical
rewind

Liberating the heart with pensive reflections
Sculpting thoughts for effective communications

Encouraging the non-vocals to vocalise
uninhibitedly
Making a fraction of the person emerge in totality

Marveling on mutual dependence for catharsis
Emancipating writers and readers from their oases

Beseeching time for their appropriate
interpretation
Letters with revelations seek unwavering attention

Dear Ma and Pa,
I trust my letter finds you in the best of health and the highest of spirits.

You must be surprised on receiving a letter from me.

I know I have been rebellious and never prompt about keeping in touch with you. Ever since I have been commissioned and posted here–you know where, I can't write more here for security reasons. I haven't written to you at all. The new life, lots of flying, studies and training have kept me busy. Although this is not a good enough reason, I would rather avoid the justifications. I will only say that I've changed; for the better, maybe? Well, you make that decision.

I am aware that you would want to know how I am, if I am eating well, sleeping well and so much more. Of course, you also would want to know if I am following the path in life that you have shown me and expect me to follow. For reasons best known to me and God, I must confess that I am enjoying this experience of an independent life, taking decisions for myself and thinking of the right and wrong. I am sorry for this disconnect and hope I am pardoned.

I admit what happened during my last leave at home is another reason. I was hurt when you did not accept the girl I had chosen for myself. In the past few months,

I have been rationalising and coming to terms with that too.

I had sent some goodies with my friend who was coming on leave and I hope you got them and liked them. The chocolates were especially for Chikki and you, ma. Tell Chikki that I miss her very much.

Despite the hurt, I think I have come to realise that we must let bygones be bygones and move forward in life. The reason for this change in heart is simple and I do believe that it is because of the lessons I have learnt during the last few months of operating in the forward areas.

My training for high altitude missions has just begun. We are getting a taste of 'real' operational flying now. The machine is being used not just for training but for missions too. We—the junior pilots or *'piloos'* as we are called, are getting to know our aircraft's limits besides our own. We carry out sorties to and from places where no normal human being would even think of going.

We land at these heights and meet the men who guard our borders all year round. These men are so happy to receive us in freezing conditions. When we land at the helipads, we find our soldiers waiting for the goodies we take for them–food, fuel and even arms and ammunition.

But the most important thing that they wait for is the small bundle that is carried under the seat of the aircraft. This bundle (of joy) contains letters from their loved ones and has taken more than a month or more to reach them.

The delight on their faces as they open the envelope addressed to them is such a wonderful sight to watch and gives us utmost satisfaction. I have now realised that this little piece of paper scrawled with a few words is worth more than its weight in gold for the recipient. I guess it gives them a sense of purpose, and also makes them attend their call of duty with renewed vigour.

And so, I have also come to realise that a letter is so very important to maintain a connection with our loved ones. Perhaps, one day in the future, we may have many other means of communication to stay in touch with our families from any corner of the world. Maybe, by then, these letters would have become a thing of the past.

I feel sorry for not being in touch and I promise you that I shall send you a letter every week from now on.

I remain, your one and only son...

Nitin

Into The 'Deep'

……… ✜ ………

What you see is not all there is
Mind delivers prescriptive kicks
As illusionary image of self swells
Chaos reigns in the critic and reveller
Reflections rise in search of purpose
Fortressing the sense of each identity
Yet bringing out connexions of all rings
With marvellously permeable precincts
Critical to the richness of all beings
Are the spectacles of intuitive thinking
Layers of visual splendour encase
The exquisiteness deeply ingrained

From up above, one can see the maze of green and brown play fields shrouded under the haze of city smoke. The massive red stone structure of the Sudan block and the silver dome of the Science Block with its big clock ticking away still look ominous.

We are training at the beautiful National Defence Academy campus and these beautiful pieces of architecture are icons of this great institution which can be seen from miles. We are atop the highest diving board at the swimming pool waiting to jump.

We didn't have much time to think from up there. If we did, we may have admired the scene better. The dark blue water at the deep end of the pool beckons.

At the Ustaad's whistle, we stand in our maroon trunks at the edge of the pool, our thin legs shaking (because of the cold shower, we would like to think) and commence climbing the fifty steps to the concrete ledge, 35 feet above the centre of the deep end of the pool.

I wonder if the others, like me, are also trying to think about the lunch at the other side of this ordeal.

The instructor has forbidden us to look down into the water. We do so anyway with a prayer on our lips. The pool looks like a blue postage stamp on a brown and green camouflage envelope. The deep end seems unfathomable even to the sunlight trying to pierce its way into its depths. All that the sun succeeds in doing is to spread a golden shimmer over the gentle waves.

The adrenaline kicks in and our hearts accelerate like an aircraft at full power for takeoff. The ramp is our runway for the moment. There is no running back now. The only way down is by taking the final leap into the deep.

The Robert Frost poem which we had just been through in our English class comes to my mind and my brain modifies it even in the panic,

The water is cold, dark and deep,
but I have to leap;
because I have promises to keep,
and there's still time before I sleep!

One step off the board and we are off—lips pursed and eyes closed shut.

The stomach churns, the eyeballs roll up, the lungs contract as if squeezing out the life in us. Hands and legs go into a grotesque dance as if trying to hold on to the thin air to stop the fall. But gravity won't have any of this, it accelerates us downwards in the few seconds that we are airborne.

And then in a moment which seems like eternity, the deep gobbles us in a thunderous splash.

The water slaps our chests and buttocks and we go under with a *whoosh*, our breath escaping in bubbles that reverberate loudly in our ears. We gasp for air, and water finds its way into our bodies—into every crevice and orifice. We sputter and choke for breath, flailing hands and legs struggling to get us to the surface of this water world.

Buoyancy takes over, and we find ourselves propelled upwards to the sunny glimmering surface of the pool. It is as if God has finally heard our prayers and is guiding us back to life. Our head pops out of the water and we try to orientate ourselves. The ordeal is almost over. We need to propel ourselves to the nearest edge of the pool and pull ourselves out.

We are alive. Yet another jump is over and done with.

Whether you are a swimmer or not, it is mandatory for cadets to jump from this height at the National Defence Academy (although in the junior terms, we jumped from a little lower, seven meters) The idea is to see if the young men have the mental courage it takes to join the military. Even if a boy is low on courage in the early years at the academy, ten meter jumps and many more of such 'mad' activities lead to build the daring and latent steel in good measure by the time the cadet passes out of the academy.

We often joke about many incidents that happened at the pool whenever we get together even now. One such incident is about Cadet 'GP'. The boy was good at everything else but hated the pool and its water. For many of us, the first jump was a waterloo—as it was for GP.

Allow me to narrate this incident in the beautiful words of my friend Flying Officer MP Anil Kumar, who narrated it to me for my book, *Born to Fly*:

> *Despite numerous commands given from below by the Divisional Officer Flt Lt Mishra, GP kept on holding to the railings on the side of the approach to the diving board. No amount of cajoling would make his grip loosen; and Nijjar—the ustaad—realised that it would be impossible to unlock the white knuckles of the boy to dislodge him from the top. Now, one fifth termer, Cadet Aggarwal, was sent to bolster the efforts to get GP to jump. A minor scuffle ensued and the boys below waited for the frail GP to now come down flying.*
>
> *Nothing of that sort happened. GP's perseverance won, and he soon managed to edge both his assailants to a drop into the pool. Aided by some un-understood law of prehensility, our man clung on to the railing, his legs dangling, a la Spiderman in his swimming costume. He then summoned energy from somewhere to do a toilsome pull-up and get back on to the seven meter board, and majestically stood there unvanquished.*

GP would have been relegated or sent home if he hadn't jumped. Eventually, jump he did and to top it all, went on to join the Indian Navy.

In life, one requires the gentle push to go into the unknown. Once you have crossed this threshold, you discover ways to get to the top. This makes you realise that one always has sufficient reserve of strength to fight adversity, come what may.

And then, as you get better at facing hardships, one continues to look for newer depths that one would want to jump into, to conquer but this time more confidently.

As young seventeen-year-olds, we had just conquered the seemingly impossible. Jumping from 35 feet only in your *chaddis* requires mettle and audacity; and sometimes—a push.

Surviving The Seniors

········ ❖ ········

*From the blanket
of firmament
the stars shine
Higher into the air
the pilot
and his bird rise
Tackling each day
a parade
of epochal events
Aware that
regular sorties
do not go as rehearsed
Overthrowing
the adversaries
our men in blue survive
With glory
they continue
to touch the skies*

CADET-15046,
GOLF SQUADRON,
NATIONAL DEFEFNCE ACADEMY,
KHADAKWASLA,
PUNE (MAHARASHTRA)

This was to be my new address for the next three years. The year was 1981 and I was barely sixteen. I had been chosen to undergo training at the National Defence Academy through one of the toughest selection processes. I was elated and on top of the world.

The boot of the Ambassador taxi had remained half open due to the size of my steel trunk that carried my world inside it, and thankfully, did not fall off during the bumpy ride. At the academy, my trunk along with a few more things were offloaded and taken to my dormitory. About a dozen or so beds were lined up in every barrack to accommodate my soon to be friends and me.

My mother was just about managing to hold back her tears, but the floodgates threatened to open as time ticked. My father, a stern army man with real war experience, would have nothing of this sentimentality for now.

It was time for a parting brief by him. He pulled me aside, forced a smile, and started the discourse in his military tenor.

'You are joining the most prestigious institution of the country. Training will start as soon as we are out of sight. Remember, it is not going to be easy at all. You will have to manage a lot of stress and learn to survive in all kinds of conditions and situations that would look unbeatable.'

He continued, 'The more difficult the task, sweeter the victory. Learn the art of survival and resilience and you will soon be flying high amongst the clouds, something that you have always wanted to do. And if you fail, there will be no one, I repeat no one but yourself to blame. Understood?' I nodded my head in confirmation.

'All the best and know that a beautiful life awaits you at the end of this.'

He hugged me close, something he hadn't done for a while, and mom and he were soon out of sight. I was on my own now, marooned in a new and seemingly hostile environment.

My mother told me later that Daddy was the one who shed the first tear after they left me.

Training, like my dad said, was tough—and tough as hell. As I look back, I really wonder how we managed to go through all that we did.

Besides the official rigmarole of drill, PT, swimming, cross country, clubs, academics and more, there was a whole lot of 'unofficial' stuff that wasn't mentioned in our timetables. I do believe that this was what made us into hardened soldiers. It was here that we mastered the art of survival too.

We had our bit of unofficial punishment or *ragda* as we would call it. As we grew 'senior' through the six terms, it petered out.

Very soon, we understood the meaning of 'being at the end of the food chain' or 'where the buck stopped' and 'lesser mortals' very clearly.

There were so many of these unofficial punishments. And there was no dearth of seniors ready to mete it out to us hapless victims.

For the smallest of 'offence' or no offence at all, or simply if your senior didn't like your face, you could be changed into '*bajri order*', 'phantom rig' or 'drill order'.

You could be made to hang on to 'seventh heaven' or undergo 'heat treatment' or a 'bathroom session'. You could be ordered to come to 'heckle' order at one instant and asked to do a 'cabin cupboard' at the other. The list was unending and an NDA cadet could write a thesis on these.

Bajri order required one to fill sand inside the backpacks and all the little attachments that made up our combat gear. Even the plastic water bottle which hung at the back was filled with sand, and, without doubt, it could weigh down the strongest.

In the Phantom rig, one was required to wear his maroon swimming trunks over the olive green dungarees and strut around the squadron aka Phantom from pygmy land.

Drill order required you to don your well starched khakis and wear the big ammunition boots, belts, anklets and berets. What the senior made you do after you reported to him in these rigs was up to his whims. He could make you run, front roll, side roll or hang from beams, do star jumps or frog leaps, push-ups, or crocodile jumps.

I particularly remember getting a badly bruised back after rolling around in my *bajri* order once, the sand kept pouring out on the floor as I rolled around. Unluckily for me, it had a fair amount of sharp gravel mixed in it and the prickly stuff did all the damage.

The worst part of these punishments was when the senior made you stand outside his room and said nothing. The waiting was killing, and once in a while he came out of his room, taking a break from whatever he was doing to give us MLs (moral lectures) which meant nothing.

Hanging on seventh heaven was to simply hang on to the seventh line of wires that made up the wire mesh above our cabins and it could be done in any rig that you were in. It was quite a sight to see someone hanging on for dear life only in his underwear or the best of formals. I would like to believe that the strengthening of the fingers which squeezed the trigger of the weapon later was achieved here.

Heat treatment was meted out in the hot sun in the balcony of the top floor of the squadron building. Shoes removed, one had to get on his hands and feet and do some bend-stretches to warm up. Just being on your bare hands and legs was bad enough. The white ceramic tiles of the balcony were designed to absorb all the solar energy that was incident on them and only too willing to transfer it to the hardening skin of our hands and feet. Cadets squirmed and writhed about, transferring their weight on each hand and legs alternatively; and the punishment, more often than not, ended up with blisters which would be troublesome for days after.

Bathroom treatment was reserved for winters. Down to your underwear, this form of Chinese torture was designed to make the victims stand under hot and cold showers alternatively and if the senior wanted more fun, he could ask us to roll, haunch and do some acrobatics on the wet and cold floor.

Some 'lighter' punishments, though heavy on the mind, were the 'heckle order' and the 'cabin cupboard'. These two were inflicted one after the other in most cases. For the heckle order, one was required to pack all belongings in the room into the trunk and be ready to leave the academy. After this, invariably, orders were given to get back the cabin to 'cabin cupboard' or inspection standards. It was disruptive, time consuming and downright annoying. These mind games also took up most of the 'relaxing' time that one had at the academy.

One only becomes wiser with age, not because someone tells you but because of going through the situations that life plays up. The punishments were physically and mentally taxing but we became stronger because of them, something we realised much later.

Not much has changed at the Academy over the years and despite all the modern gadgetry and outlook, I hope these little *ragdas* are still in vogue and making our future soldiers as tough as we need them to be to fight our enemies.

The Siachen Soldier

White expanses of many feet of snow
Some solid patches, some just hollow
Braving the hypothermic conditions
Valiant soldiers don't lose their gusto
They know they have to keep moving
Come any dust, thunder or hailstorm
Even in temperatures much below zero
Their fervour to serve the nation grows
Enduring even the atmospheric freeze
Their hearts continue to beat strongly
Habitual to the inhospitable neighbours
White blanket is just another terrain

Aa Chal ke Tujhe mai le ke chalu... (Film *Door Gagan Ki Chhaon Mein,* 1964)

In the stillness of the night, the lyrics of this song at the back of my mind keep me entertained. I imagine the musicians accompanying me while I hum this song-karaoke style. The images of the hero and heroine running around trees against the ornate splash of flowers under a dizzy blue sky are a treat to my closed eyes. Once a while, I transpose myself into being the hero, chasing the heroine and catching her, swooping her into my arms for a romantic kiss.

A waft of cold freezing air leaks in from somewhere while the wind howls its usual whine outside, speeding through the snow and earth covered valleys of the higher Himalayas. It gets me out of my reverie and I promise myself to do something about this the first thing in the morning. The only thing to do for now is to put your head completely inside the sleeping bag to avoid being bitten by the minus thirty-seven degrees freeze.

I breathe in the stale smell of my sleeping bag mixed with fumes of kerosene, smoke and of course, my sweat and grime. I think of the sun bathed yellow *sarson ke khet* (mustard fields) and the fresh air of my village and these smells and scenes take my thoughts to another song.

Kya hua tera vada (Film *Hum Kisi se Kam Nahi*-1977) starts to ring in my ears.

Nothing patriotic but only romantic. The notes ring clear in my ears, as I snuggle for warmth in this 24/7 temporary shelter made of tin and rocks which I call home.

The stars are still out there shining ever so bright as they do here, without any resistance of the atmospheric haze and smoke. There are still a few more hours to get ready for my duty.

And what is my duty?

Simply stand under a tin shed with my weapon pointing at the enemy. If they dare come this way, I shall cut them to ribbons. But they haven't, so far, and hopefully won't. When they did so in Kargil, we gave them a bloody nose, didn't we? All of us love our life, except of course, the maniacs.

Once in a while, we keep each other awake with a few bursts of shells and rounds from our light machine gun. The firing gets intense especially when there is an India-Pakistan cricket match. Fun and games start between sparring partners on this field too.

In my rock and tin bunker at 18,000 feet, the few weeks spent here seem like eternity. I can just about see the enemy camp right across from where I am. These guys have better connectivity with the road almost reaching their camps. Not like the road to my bunker which ends at the base camp situated miles away, 8000 feet below.

For reaching my home from this 'road head,' we all had to go through rough and rigorous training to get used to the heights, temperatures and terrain. After that, it was trudging through waist deep snow, climbing ice walls and going across crevasses and braving blizzards in addition to acclimatising in stages at various heights and reaching this bunker called home.

The fun part of the training at the base camp was to learn to ride snow scooters. All these preparations made mountaineers out of us, but I am sure it will help us survive where even the breath seems to freeze in your lungs.

We are almost 5000 of us, sprinkled across the glaciated area, guarding an imaginary blurred line that only the cartographer and the people in Delhi know of and fight over. What I know for sure is my area of responsibility and the arc of fire of my weapon. I do my bit as ordered by my superiors, that's all.

There will be a chopper coming in early morning. The snow in the evening has obliterated the helipad markings. I have to open a few tins of coffee to mark the **H** (place for them to land). Some improvisation of *rangoli* art this is. Speaking of coffee, I will need to melt some snow over my *Bukhari* to make myself a hot cup too. To awaken one's bowels from slumber at this altitude and temperature, a cup of coffee or tea is a must before one heads to the 'thunder-boxes'. These are simply holes in the snow over which a makeshift commode is made to do your morning thing.

Oh, I haven't told you what a *Bukhari* is. It is a large rustic kerosene heater whose metal skin burns bright red through night and day, trying hard to keep us warm. It is common to have minor mishaps of *Bukharis* exploding, or spewing carbon-monoxide inside our shanties. That's the reason our home smells of smoke and kerosene—a smell that we absorb into our DNA by the time we end our tenure here.

Rations here are aplenty. We are stocked for six months. The helicopters are our lifeline. The small ones land with their miniscule loads while the bigger ones just drop their large packets by parachute and go away. I love the small ones which we refer to as *macchar* (mosquito). Besides seeing new faces and being in touch with the real world through the brave pilots who fly them in, we also get fresh fruits, vegetables and most importantly, letters from home. The *macchar* caters to our emergent requirements of medicines, fuel and ammunition too.

Sometimes, when we are sick and need evacuation, the fastest way down to hospital is by this chopper. I remember just recently, we had an accident where my friend received a grievous injury due to a fall during enemy bombing. The chopper came, took him to Leh and within a few hours the man was at a hospital in Chandigarh—saved.

And when the choppers come, the noise travels to the other side too. The enemy doesn't spare a moment to welcome them with a barrage of artillery shells. These projectiles come whistling in through the sparse air, crashing into the snow and ice, making black pockmarks without exploding.

God only knows how many unexploded bombs lie freezing around here.

The parachutes along with their loads thrown by the

big choppers keep lying around the camp area where they have landed till the time we need something. It is like going shopping to the mall for us.

Nothing can go bad or rot here in this chill, even dead bodies remain preserved for months. The strings and cords of the used parachutes are used to weave hammocks and swings—an expertise that has been passed down generations. It is a good way to pass time and also make a good gift for friends and family back home. The cloth of the parachute is used for a multitude of things. It is tough and serves to cover our bunkers too. I must remember to get some of this cloth to cover the hole that is causing the cold wind to enter my bunker.

Food is mostly tinned and not appetising. We eat only to survive, not to look after our taste buds anyway. Precooked cauliflowers, carrots, beans, potatoes and what not comes in these tins. Even the roti comes packed in sealed containers. By the way, we are told that the cost of providing one single roti in the glacier in 1985 was 21 rupees. It must be costing hundreds now. A fair amount of tax payer's money goes into looking after us here.

Additionally, we have these emergency rations called 'Meals Ready to Eat' or 'MRE' in short, which are more edible than the tinned stuff. *Dal Makhani, Chicken Masala, Palak Paneer, Pulao* and such exotic dishes come in sealed silvery packets. Just put these into boiling water and the meal is ready. Our favourite food however, has remained 'Maggi' noodles. Noodles when boiled with milkmaid and water with a bit of butter garnished with oodles of dry fruits makes good kheer. The masala sachets of the noodles go into hot butter to make *tadka* (tempering) for our *daal*. The egg powder is first made into omelets and the same are boiled in the *daal* giving us egg curry. Over time, the inhabitants of these bunkers have resorted to many such innovations and improvisations that one could write a cook book on.

When the pilots land here, they are welcomed with a glass of hot water and a cup of tea and *pakodas*—all of which have a smoky-kerosene flavour. The pilots don't complain at all and happily eat whatever we offer them. We look upon them as gods and angels of mercy and are so happy to greet and meet them.

Dry fruits and chocolates are in plentiful. The dry fruits go into almost everything that we cook to make it *shahi* (royal), and yes, I have an interesting story about the chocolates to tell.

My bed is made on piles of chocolates covered with a ply board. The rats, big ones, come at night and nibble away on this sweet. Every now and then, a layer below is eaten away and I have to raise the level of my bed with another layer of chocolates. The rats survive well in these freezing conditions as do cockroaches.

We also have pet dogs here who are our best friends. They walk up with us from base camp and stay with us in our tenure, only to return with the new set of men who come to replace us. I spend a lot of time talking to our dog Sheru, who never complains of the cold nor cribs about living conditions. You see, there is a thing or two to learn about survival in the cold from these creatures too.

It is morning and the first rays of the sun are brightening the eastern skies. The long shadows of our hill keep the enemy territory in darkness for the time being. The process will reverse in the evening around 4 o'clock. Darkness descends early and the cold becomes colder once the sun vanishes behind these mountains.

The evenings, sometimes, are dull and dreary leading to bouts of boredom and homesickness. We try and keep ourselves entertained with music and watch videos on our otherwise 'dead' mobiles. Calls to home can be made in emergency on the only satellite phone available—a gadget that has come in recently and helped to improve our morale.

As part of rest and recuperation, we play cricket, perform yoga on ice, sing songs and celebrate every occasion and festival in the book. There are no such pigeonholes as caste, creed, religion, language or colour, we accept each other, making inseparable bonds for life.

I am ready to perform my duty for the next four hours. I hope to remember to wear my gloves to avoid getting burnt by the cold metal of the weapon and the shed. A few days ago, my hand got stuck to the freezing muzzle of my weapon, and the cold burnt through the skin of my palm, hurting for days.

On guard for two hours, I think, I whistle, and hum a tune waiting for time to pass. It seems that time too has frozen here; two hours is a long long time.

Life continues with amazing regularity while we count the days left to get back to humanity. The cold and the lack of oxygen is sure to affect me in the long run. I am told that living in these freezing conditions where temperatures go as low as minus 40 could lead to memory loss, an oversensitive stomach and premature greying.

When I go home on leave after this stint, I shall impress my whole village with the stories of my adventures in this freezer. I plan to arrive home with my long unkempt hair, wiry beard, bushy moustache and blackened lips for effect. The only thing that I won't be able to show them is how the breath froze into ice on my whiskers.

It would take a long time for us, physically and mentally, to get back to 'normal' thawed life.

I am the Siachen Soldier and am proud to serve our country the way I do.

Proud Flier

In this globe we call our world
We are but transient beings
Moving between dust and shadows
Dreaming of plenty and bravado
Everything that we ultimately do
Is to give our abodes a warm hue
As we meet and greet a guest or two
Temporariness of locus ensues
As search for enlightenment thrives
'Tis time to spread our wings and fly

I am the Mi-8 helicopter. Born in Russia in the late '70s, purchased for the Indian Air Force in early '80s, I have been flapping my rotors all over India's nook and cranny since then. I may be old, but I am still very reliable. Weighing 12 tons and more when filled to capacity, you can take a ride with me and travel about 400 to 500 km on a full tank. You would get shaken (but not stirred aka James Bond) when you fly with me since I vibrate a lot, but I assure you that you will love the ride and remember me forever. And most importantly, I could be a life saver, taking you or picking you up from any remote corner of the country; the only thing I would need is a small flat piece of land for me to put my legs down.

Besides giving a lift to many—more often than not—I carry food, ammunition and all those things that our troops require inside my big cabin for their comfort and sustenance. It is good to see the happy faces of the soldiers who guard our frontiers when I land amongst them. Most importantly, I also carry letters and parcels from their families—it keeps their morale sky high.

Many a time, I am tasked to carry VIP guests, and these missions are special. From heads of state to film stars, politicians, civil servants and the likes, I have carried them all. When the President of Pakistan was in

India in 2001, I carried him to Agra where he saw the Taj Mahal and then to Ajmer Sharif and Jaipur to watch the India-Pakistan cricket match. Many guests take rides with me to go to far flung areas like Gangotri, Yamnotri, Badrinath, Kedarnath, Tawang, Leh, Ladhakh etc. I save their time and energy and make their treacherous and rough rides over long distances easy. At other times, some guests are taken to the border outposts to meet the troops and these are missions that I personally love.

My most special guest, however, has been Dr APJ Abdul Kalam, our former President, who flew inside me many a time. What an amazing and down to earth man he was!

Whilst my insides reek of onions, oil, kerosene and animal dung most of the time, I undergo a metamorphosis for the VIP travel.

The ground crew cleans me up thoroughly with soap and water and gives me a touch-up paint job so that all the blemishes that I have acquired in my hitherto rough rides are taken care of. Once that is done, carpets are rolled out on my floor and things start getting cozy inside. Large recliner seats—which have seen better days flying in the 'Maharaja' first class cabins—are then fitted on to the cabin floor. Curtains adorn the small round windows and seats are covered in white and magazines placed in their pockets. The entire atmosphere inside the cabin is now transformed and looks alluring for my guests who are venturing out to their destinations.

A portable larder is stowed away on board. It is

handled by the flight gunner during these short flights. We have everything that would make our guests feel wanted and comfortable—soft drinks, sodas, small eats, dry fruits, chocolates, mouth fresheners and the works. Before the guests arrive, the flight gunner will spray the insides with some sweet-smelling aerosol and I am then fit to receive a king.

And my crew is specially selected to fly the VIP guests. With years of experience and special training for these kinds of missions, they are adept at making sure that the rides are as smooth as possible. Wearing special white overalls, (unlike the blue greasy ones they wear on normal missions) they make heads turn with their peak caps, accoutrements, and their 'aviator' sunglasses. I, for one, have seen many a young lass swooning over them.

Before they fly me, every small detail of the mission will be discussed threadbare. There is no room for error of any kind. The 'DOT,' or 'Door Opening Time' has to be correct to the second and the crew takes pride in achieving it. VIP trips are generally short and sweet since I am tasked with only the last mile connectivity. The guests arrive at the nearest airport in their special planes and then board me for the flight. Most of them are nice people and very courteous to speak to. They often pose along with my pilots in front of me for a photo. I am sure that many of my photos adorn living rooms across the globe.

After all, when I fly these missions, I become an instrument of diplomacy and good relations, enhancing the image of our country and the Indian Air Force. Therefore, no effort is spared to make my guests feel special. The remarks made by those who have flown with me are a testimony to this. The guest books have signatures of the likes of Indira Gandhi, Brezhnev, Nelson Mandela, Queen Elizabeth and many more.

I am aware that I will be retired from service soon and replaced with a modern machine. Along with my memories, I too, shall soon be part of history—rested but never forgotten.

The Metal Bird

········ ✦ ········

As long as the hearts keeping pumping
And warmth in their veins keeps moving
They may be allowed to rest on one leg
But there's no tolerance for a square peg
Individual threads of the nest are brittle
Combined strength can be doubted little
Forces holding 'em together are internal
Bonds made at nascent stage are eternal
When clarion call is heard in the nation
At once they provide aid to that station
Despite adversities vigour they conjure
To ensure their nest is evermore secure

Some birds are born in nests but I am assembled in a factory—bit by bit, part by part. A million wires run through my nervous system. I have a designer metal body that houses the engines that propel me to fly and soar, because that is what I am meant for, and that is what I like the best. I am the metal bird and my nest is the hangar that I am made in and subsequently nestle in for the rest of my life.

The covers are coming off slowly and I can feel them sliding off my smooth skin. I feel the cool air and shiver. It is still time to daylight, but I am used to this early awakening by the ground crew almost every day. Once they uncover me, my panels are opened and I express my anguish with a creak, groan and a clank. Men with torches clamber all over me and check out the multitude of tubes, wires, pipes and aluminum that make up my insides. Each of these guys have their tasks cut out. While one checks the electrics, the other checks my hydraulics and yet another the engines. Soon, all systems are checked and I am good to go. I am refueled, greased, oiled, and charged and ready for yet another day in the sky.

A tractor strolls into the hangar with a rattling towing arm bouncing behind it that is attached to my front wheels. With an initial tug and a jerk, I move. We start rolling along the yellow line which will lead us into the parking bay. I am the heavier one, and very soon, one won't be able to tell if the tractor is doing the pulling or I, the pushing. But as of now, he is the boss and he parks me in the bay with my nose wheel over the white roundel meant for it. He then returns to the nest to get my other sisters who have also gone through the same morning routine as I have.

With the first rays of sunlight peeping over the horizon, all of us immaculately parked gleaming machines present a picture for a postcard.

The pilots will soon walk out of the crew room after their briefings and come fly us. The weather is beautiful and the early morning ride promises to be smooth—no bumps, no birds and nothing that can stop me from cutting smoothly through the air. I always enjoy these first sorties of the day.

And yes, I do have a busy schedule. Different sets of pilots fly me as I take to the skies three to four times a day. And if there are night assignments, add another two or three flights. Night flying sorties are so cool—no harsh manoeuvring, just simple turns and gentle climbs.

We need to work hard, my sisters and I. After all, we have a national security task at hand. Our young pilots will soon graduate to bigger, sophisticated, and mightier birds designed to kill. They will use all that they have learnt here to kill birds who are not of our feather and flock—a task that requires stronger and fitter machines.

I too need to be maintained well to remain fit. To look after our overall welfare, we have a big-boss who has an office in the nest. He plans and plots our maintenance, utilisation, and ensures that spares for us are requisitioned in time. He also ensures that the number of hands needed to keep me well fed, oiled, greased and serviced are always available, so that I can take on the tasks at hand with assurance. I need my parts changed on time. Can't have failures in flight, can we? No roadside assistance there.

Once in a while, after I have done my bit of aviating, I need to go back to another nest. This nest is different from the one I live in, and is more like a multi-speciality hospital. It has all the instruments and labs needed to check me thoroughly. And while all the worn-out gaskets, seals and other parts are replaced, I get time to rest and recuperate. Once a while, I have landed up with major problems and leaks and I had to be stripped to the bone. The good part is that parts among us birds are interchangeable; and therefore, they get me fit and declare me fly-worthy in time, as per schedule.

My typical day is full of turns and twists, both literally and figuratively. The pilots throw me around and test my limits. And when they do that, my joints creak with the excessive forces on my body. Sometimes, it is a bad landing which gives me sore tires and an oily oleo. Back on ground, I need time to re-energise. My tanks are filled to their capacity. Gases and oils are checked and topped up as required. This short and sweet break between sorties is rejuvenating and soon, I am in the air again, enjoying the wind passing over my wings.

As flying for the day gets over, the tractor is back with its yellow towing arm. Soon, I will be back in the cozy confines of my nest for the night. But before I go to sleep, they need to do a 'LFS' (Last Flight Servicing) on me and put my covers back on. The hangar soon becomes dark, and so does my cockpit; and the humdrum of the day fades into the quiet of the night.

I lie waiting silently for another beautiful morning when the covers will come off again.

In a few years from now, I would have lived my life in the air and could be grounded permanently or ground to dust. I, for one, am optimistic that I would be chosen to be hoisted on a stand and festooned to the ground, away from my nest, living the rest of my life under the skies, on public display. And maybe, birds of the feathered kind will come perch on my wings and tell me about of their days spent flying, reminding me of my own good-old-days!

My Cockpit My Home

.... ✤ ....

I carry my heart and life wisdom wherever I go
A canvas tent or stalks of hay can be my home
Trenches deep, snow heaps or branches of trees
Minimal resources I use to create cozy zones
Where you cannot dare to imagine life
I stay put to establish for you an environ secure
Scraped by barbs of boundaries and adversaries
I am stationed on every border for your life
Whilst you go about your routine and sleep at ease
I protect our nation from the hostile breeze

Home is where the heart is and mine lies in the cockpit of my aircraft. That's where it beats best, that's where it gets the power to beat on and on. Even later in life, if someone asks me about the most comfortable place in this world, the answer would be the same —the small confines of this home. Here, once you are strapped in, you become an integrated whole—a perfect blend of man and machine.

Let me take you on a tour of my home. Let me show you what happens in my home. Not many of you have been there before, right?

The cockpit is like my playroom; I get to operate and play with a number of gizmos and gadgets. Through them, I get to have complete control over my machine, make it do what I want it to. But before I got into the real cockpit, I practiced many hours in a dummy cockpit.

The earliest dummy cockpit was created by us cadets at the Air Force Academy in 1983. In those days, there were no simulators or mock up cockpits available for training. Young men were forced to rely on innovative skills that had been passed down through generations. A dummy cockpit was needed to get familiar with the new environment that wannabe pilots were to soon get into, and also to learn checks and procedures in lower risk environs.

It was a must to know each and every switch and instrument in the cockpit before one got to the skies. An interesting exercise or 'test' that was to be passed before any cadet got to fly was called the 'blind fold check'. The cadet sat blindfolded inside the cockpit and the instructor called out the switches and dials; Altimeter, Air Speed Indicator, Radio, Undercarriage, Flaps. The cadet had to point towards the place where the dial or switch was located. Not easy, but doable with a lot of practice.

And to practice for this, the dummy cockpit came handy. A cardboard was cut in the shape of the instrument console and some of the other switches and dials too. With coloured pencils, we maxed out our artistic aptitude to sketch shapes of switches and dials as realistically as possible. This work of art was then hung on a wall and a study-chair placed in front became the pilot's seat. Other cutouts were placed on the left and right of the chair and the 'cockpit' was ready. A hockey stick came in handy to serve as the joystick while two shoe boxes served as rudder pedals.

Usually, post dinner, we would don our helmets, put our visors down and get into the dummy cockpit to practice the checks and procedures written in the checklists. But there was one little hitch, when the cadet wore the oxygen mask over his mouth, it became difficult to breathe since the valve at the end of the O2 tube didn't open unless connected to the oxygen system of the aircraft. But this too was resolved with innovative means. A matchstick did the trick. It was used to jam the valve in open position.

Enough of these snatches from history. Let's get into the real cockpit.

This home, like any other home is expensive to buy and live in. But since it is company owned, all one needs to do is to treat it well and follow the set drills that have been taught for safe living. The punishment for not following the house rules can be severe, and one could be evicted permanently if one doesn't follow them in letter and spirit.

This home is fully air-conditioned (it always was, right from the days the Wright Brothers flew the first one) and hermetically sealed, keeping you safe even from a nuclear or biological fallout. A battery of men and women work hard to keep the insides and outsides clean and all gizmos working satisfactorily.

When airborne, the view from the windows and the glass dome of the cockpit is exhilarating.

There is no furniture in this home except for the sophisticated motorised chair that you sit on. It can be moved in all directions to make sure that you are comfortable and can control the activities of your home while sitting right there. When you go aviating in this home, you are always aware of what all the parts and systems of the airplane are up to. You can monitor parameters like temperatures, pressures, RPMs, and the very heartbeat of your machine. Can't have any system misbehaving, can you?

The mind of the modern cockpits is the computer, which controls and monitors almost everything that happens in here. It also ensures that you treat this abode well and do not exceed any of the specified limits. It records all that happens in and around your home and makes it available to ground staff on landing. Thanks to the computer, it is easier to be warned when you do something wrong or forget to do something important.

In some of the Russian aircraft of the older generation (some of them are still in use today), a house-keeping system called '*Natasha*' monitored the working of critical systems. When something went wrong, Natasha was programmed to warn the crew about the emergent situation in her sing song voice and also tell them what needed to be done.

'High vibrations left engine, Main hydraulic system fail, Emergency fuel reserve....'

Sometimes, things can go horribly wrong and you may be forced to escape from the confines of your home. The seat can be ejected out of the cockpit by just pulling a handle if one needs to abandon ship. Thereafter, a sequence of events will ensure that you come down to Mother Earth hanging from a parachute while your home is smashed to smithereens.

All situations need not force you to leave the confines of your home in this manner. When minor failures or problems occur, you—as head of the home—are expected to take appropriate action and get your home back on ground in one piece.

Your cockpit does not have a kitchen or a loo. Often, when one undertakes long duration missions, you carry your food in your pockets and munch it on the way. During such flights, you may need to wear diapers too, and attend the call of nature right on your seat.

In helicopters and transport aircraft, things are slightly different. They have sitting rooms, galleys, and toilets for the guests. Guests can have a comfortable and smooth ride in their seats. Most of you readers would have had that experience, I am sure.

And you have a boss who controls you while you do FRCS (flying around the countryside) in your home. While you aviate, the Air Traffic Control and the radars exercise 'remote' control over you and see that you do not cross the limit of your bounds.

The modern-day cockpits are different akin to modern constructs. The yesteryear dials and meters have been replaced by dark glass panels. Once you power up, the switches and instruments are projected electronically on these touch screens. You could shift the instruments the way you like to see them just as you do on the touch screens of your mobile. All information is now literally available on a touch of your fingertips.

On a lighter note, I wish I would be able to see some videos on the dark screens whilst on long missions, especially when things get boring when flying on autopilot controlled by my computer and my seat can be pushed back and tilted to relax for a while.

But I think I have done well even without these luxuries. From being alert, following rules, managing many systems and controls so as to get the optimum performance of my machine and making do with what I had, the cockpit taught me so much. It also taught me about the fragility of life and the need to be content, no matter what.

Now that I am permanently out of the cockpit, it is time to put into use what I have learnt in my new home made of bricks and mortar.

Landing Happy

.... ✦ ....

Every day I take off with my bird
Both clutching the other's control
We rise above the dust we upset
Prepared for any unexpected test

We traverse many urban landscapes
Also to farms and hills we escape
We rule the air and streets below
Fancying even to roads narrow

Though we respect the elements
I'm aware of my bird's temperament
Nerves of steel we literally have
Every opportunity to fly we grab

'254 finals, three greens, full flaps'
– '254 Cleared to land. Winds 10 O' Clock 5 knots'

This is a night flying sortie and an eerie glow of the instruments fills the cockpit as I look to align myself to the runway. I get clearance to land when I am around 700 feet above the ground and should, God and aircraft willing, be on terra-firma a few seconds from now.

The two lines of lights along the runway edges are like diamonds that shine through the dark haze helping me align my aircraft for a touchdown. As I descend on the glide-path towards the touchdown point, the lights separate and become parallel lines meeting at infinity. The adrenaline that kicked in some time ago, keeps me alert and aware of what is happening in and around the aircraft. One mistake in these final stages, no matter how small, can prove costly, both for the man and the machine.

I have now fallen in love with this street where I aviate from in good and bad times to fly a multitude of missions to keep our skies safe. I love it, though it has no trees, no houses except for the ATC building half-way down, and some soft ground filled with sand at both ends; not to forget the Arrester Barrier at the ends of the runway, ready to arrest my aircraft if my brakes give up on me during landing or if I must abort my takeoff for any reason.

Every time I return from a mission, it is always a joy to see the runway from afar. This elongated rectangular piece of hard concrete invites and beckons me; reassuring me that it will always be my home, my street—somewhere I will always belong.

Once a while, in bad weather or poor visibility, or when one is literally lost, this street can also become all elusive. While looking for it using all possible means, panic unsettles the best of the best. I am sure there isn't a pilot who hasn't had this feeling at some point in his aviating career. However much one may enjoy flying and feel at home in the cockpit, the glimmer of the lights at the edge of the runway puts a pilot at ease and there's nothing like touching down on solid ground and the squeal of tyres touching concrete.

Pilots work hard in preparation for a planned mission. To ensure zero error, we study the maps in detail, go over the additional checks, procedures and drills specific to the mission, and revise emergency actions to be ready for contingencies.

Then, before the pilot strides to the aircraft, a detailed briefing on the boards and charts ensures there are no lingering doubts. After this, the pilot will sign for the mission in the 'Flight Authorization Book', or the 'Form-700' to take over the aircraft. The '700', as it is called, contains the history of the aircraft and the details of the servicing carried out and this is where the technicians sign confirming that the aircraft is technically fit to fly.

Walking to the aircraft with a helmet tucked under the arms, an oxygen mask draped like a snake over the shoulders, the pilot mulls over the sortie to be flown. The silent aircraft awaits in the parking bay along with the ground crew. The pilot does a quick run through check of maps, survival kit, weapon, first aid kit, and all such knick-knacks that go into the many pockets of his flying overalls.

With helmet resting on the aircraft wing, the pilot wears oil-and-grease-stained chamois leather gloves, and goes around the aircraft carrying out a pre-flight inspection caressing the machine at its nerve points, caressing the skin much like what a rider does before mounting his horse.

Climbing sprightly into the cockpit with the help of the ladder positioned, the pilot jumps in, legs straddling the joy stick, quickly scanning around for foreign objects. The feet instinctively go to the rudder pedals. The parachute filled hard seat is familiar. Instinctively from training, the pilot picks up the straps and is helped by the ground crew to secure them around the shoulders, and is soon snug in the machine strapped to his parachute.

With the helmet on and the oxygen and mikes connected, the man-machine integration is complete. The pilot is one with the aircraft now.

The pilot now gets to work inside the cocooned environment.

With a shudder, the engine whines to life and the aircraft awakens from its slumber. The instrument needles yaw and stretch, some lights flash in the cockpit while some go off as they should.

The chocks on the wheels are removed and the aircraft is given a final check by the technicians on tarmac. With a loud whine from the engine, the aircraft lurches forward along the taxiway. The nose bucks in as the pilot checks the brakes as if to salute the technicians who got the aircraft ready for flight.

The aircraft traverses a few narrow lanes before reaching the runway. Lined up on the centerline of the runway, I feel that I am standing at one end of a long foot-rule. The white unbroken lines on the sides and the broken lines along the centre merge into the haze and seem to lead into the skies above.

The adrenaline kicks in. The pilot does a quick rehearsal of actions for abandoning takeoff or ejecting out of the airplane due to unforeseeable circumstances and once all is set, he asks the ATC permission for take-off.

And when the ATC replies 'cleared for takeoff', it is like the red traffic light going green after a long wait. With full power on, the pilot will check his instruments one last time before he releases the brakes.

The machine surges forward with the bountiful energy from the engines.

The feeling of being pushed backwards into the seat, this power and acceleration is unlike anything else I have felt.

Pelting down the runway, when I lift the machine off the ground, I feel like Bach's Jonathan Livingstone Seagull.

Oh, ecstasy! Pure ECSTASY.

THE 'HOOD'

········ ❖ ········

Nobody ever became a pilot by just wanting to be
Pining to spread their wings to become the machine

Training can't reach realms where intuition can be
Though one might kick the tyres and light the fires
The inferno inside can only be ignited in sobriety

As CAVU, 5 by 5 or butter landing can't be a surety
Equipment could fail despite their preflight scrutiny
Situation in the hood cannot be simulated in totality

Ultimately what counts is experience and dexterity
To accomplish the mission despite every difficulty
Hood closed, Pressurisation ON.

Before we readied for take-off, this was what we had to call out. It meant that the glass bubble canopy of the small jet trainer aircraft was shut and secure. We were now completely cocooned inside the airplane, and this would be our little world for the rest of the sortie.

What then, did the hood mean for us pilots?

As pilots, we are taught to fly the machine by the instruments in the cockpit, so that, we can safely navigate through bad weather and poor visibility. Of course, the modern jet fighters and airliners of today have an extra 'virtual' pilot called the 'auto pilot'—a set of electronic gizmos which can get the aircraft back on terra-firma, without the inputs of the human pilot. An autopilot is designed to take away a fair amount of workload of physically flying the machine. But, in the '80s when we learnt to fly, such automated systems were yet not fitted on our primitive machines we flew during our training, and, we had to learn to fly the aircraft physically by using the references provided by our instruments.

Our position in three dimensions is determined by our senses and if one doesn't have a clear horizon or cannot see anything outside, one may end up in 'unusual attitudes.' and take the aircraft into dangerous regimes; ending in a pile of metal and rubber if one does not know how to recover from the situation. There have been so many instances in aviation when pilots have lost their sense of orientation and ended up flying inverted too. Sounds impossible? It is true. Ask any pilot and he will confirm the fact.

So how did we learn how to fly on instruments?

We used the HOOD of course!

This hood was different, however. It was a hood to cover the hood (Canopy) that I spoke about. It was basically a dark curtain which went across the canopy bubble and the wind shield of the aircraft thereby obscuring the external view, forcing us to look at the instruments and we were to take cues from them to control the aircraft. The instructor on the other hand, was able to look outside and was fully 'visual' and in control of the situation if we got into trouble. He took us through the exercises of putting the aircraft into unusual attitudes (even inverted sometimes) and asked us to recover it to safety.

During these manoeuvres, the heart would beat faster and the brain gave us wrong signals about how we were placed in the three dimensions of space. In this confusion, one was inclined to disbelieve the instruments.

But the intent of the exercise was to train us to learn to believe the instruments and recover the aircraft safely.

Without any visual reference, it would be difficult to control any machine, or for that matter, even walking on ground without falling! If I were to tell you to drive your car on a straight road by just seeing the speedometer and a compass or GPS, would you be able to? It would be difficult as well as stressful. Imagine doing that in the skies with an aircraft and its occupants dependent on you.

By and by, we got comfortable under the hood and the instructor became confident that we could fly the airplane to some degree of accuracy without external references. As we got more proficient to fly on instruments, we could improve our 'instrument rating' from 'white' to 'green' to 'master green', which simply put, meant that the higher rated pilot could fly in worst conditions of weather.

Having been there and done that, and reflecting on the learnings of this exercise, I have come to realise that we could extrapolate the same in real life too.

For instance, if we lose our grip of life situations and the million inputs that our brain synthesises, it would become impossible to think straight and take correct decisions. We would be going around like zombies, or like an airplane in an unusual attitude, or perhaps like untethered ships without power, or like kites spinning out of control, strings severed.

People who go under their hoods without practice are the oblivious ostriches, they do not understand the situation they are in and end up in disaster.

So before you think of getting under a HOOD, make sure that you are well oriented. Practice when the days are good and bright. Who knows, tomorrow you may be caught up in a vicious storm and end up in an unusual attitude, unable to recover yourself?

Think about it.

Perspective In Flying

········ ✤ ········

From ground to the view from stratosphere
The world appears different from each layer
From micro to macro we traverse every day
Be it the journey inside or outside we essay
In the process, new realms at times we chase
Leaving toxic dumps of the past in alien space
What's seen by one could be visible to none
That's how differently the same view is spun
We mark our territories with intricate fences
To explore around and gain from experiences
Clouded in our thoughts we forever remain
Losing perspectives of others in the bargain

Perspective In Flying

The initial part of my flying training is on and my instructor and I are in our twin seater jet cockpit. He is at his wits end for a reason beyond my comprehension.

I am still trying to come to grips with operating in this new medium called 'air' and the feeling of movement in all the dimensions, all at once, perturbs me a bit. He should understand my predicament *na*? After all, he too wasn't born with wings.

On the positive side, I will soon get used to the whimsical instructors and their moods. Just like this new environment, I am sure, I shall soon be soaring like Jonathan Livingston Seagull and be an instructor like him.

My instructor has lost his mind trying to explain what is called 'perspective' in the business of flying. I, for one, like so many of my friends, have a faint idea about it, but haven't been able to grasp the meaning in totality.

'See how the runway looks from here?' he starts all over again.

He makes the aircraft climb a few thousand feet higher. 'Now look at the runway. How does it look now?' he asks again.

'It looks smaller, sir,' I say jubilantly.

'So now you understand what is perspective?'

There is a pregnant pause.

'I think perspective means how the runway appears to you from different heights. But I still haven't understood what is "correct perspective!"' I tell him, frowning behind my helmet visor.

'Uff! Uff! UFFFFFF! You are a real MUTT! Wish I could just throw you out of here now!' He takes over the machine and doles out punishment as only he can—he throws the airplane around and carries out some stomach churning manoeuvres before we go in for a landing.

And while we roll and loop around, I visualise that I am tumbling down in space after he throws me out of the cockpit. What will be the perspective as I approach close to Mother Earth, I wonder? Maybe I will learn what this all means just before I die.

We are on the final approach to land. He wakes me out of my downward tumble.

'Notice the perspective at the top of final approach and maintain the same till landing so that you will achieve the correct glide path, height and speed ratio. This is the correct perspective! Remember it all the time, you will never go wrong with your landing if your perspective is correct,' he adds.

A profound statement for life, I think. Yet, I am still at a loss as to how the perspective won't change when I come closer to land… am too involved in the landing than looking at his darn 'perspective' and let his explanation sail over my head. Befuddled, I decide to go to the dictionary in my room to check what it says. Google has not made its heyday yet.

I read slowly from the fat book, *'The art of representing three dimensional objects on a two-dimensional surface so as to give the right impression of their height, width, depth and position in relation to each other.'*

'A particular attitude towards, or way of regarding something; a point of view... outlook, view, viewpoint, point of view or stance...'

I think my instructor meant a little of both. I remain as confused as ever.

I go through the rigours of training, go solo and become a qualified pilot myself. Years later, one day, whilst I am aviating, the meaning of the word finally dawns.

I am flying very high over Mother Earth—all I can see is the exquisiteness of the land below me. The beautiful mountains, rivers and the plains and the green countryside dotted with little homes. They all seem to merge into one beautiful landscape.

But as I get closer, I start seeing the micro view. The imperfections of the earth, the trees and the winding roads and rivers. And when I am down on ground, I get to observe people, traffic, dirt, rich, poor, good, bad and the ugly. I see and understand things clearly when I get closer to them, and that includes humans too.

I get down from my aircraft and walk towards the crew room, deep in thought.

There is an anthill near our unit complex and I stop to look at what is happening here. There are zillions of them, these little creatures—oblivious about everything else but themselves. Even about the five-and-a-half-foot giant towering over them. They are at work and it is time for them to gather food and make their homes tidy.

From their viewpoint, the anthill is their mountain, home and world. Everything else does not matter.

I think of the millions of atoms and cells that make up an ant, or for that matter, everything in this world. My thoughts now move into outer space and I see how the Earth looks rotating in the solar system. It must really seem like an ant to the Sun. Maybe, when compared to the entire universe, our little solar system with its planets would look like an atom with little electrons moving around them, but they hold a world in themselves.

I am getting too philosophical. Maybe it is time to get myself back to being just me.

Anything and everything can be viewed differently due to different perspectives, right? What is big for some is small for others, richness for some is poverty for others, beauty to some is ugliness to others etc.

Everything is relative in life because of perception.

The micro and macro—that's perspective.

Fueling Man and Machine

.... ✧ ....

On many a spontaneous mission we launch
We do not take to the skies just for a jaunt
Our engines whine if we do not get our fill
Even smallest chores then appear uphill
Adequate fuel our bodies and tanks want
Unit cafeterias are, thus, our preflight haunts
Mandatorily, on air-crew meal we must feed
To cater to basic on-flight metabolic needs
Cafes are also a place for aviation conversations
From targets, tumbleweeds, trajectories and trails
To shadows, saunters, sandwiches and scrambles
Debates on R.O.A.D. ahead may also find
mentions
Banters of dynamic aviators enliven the place
Vibes and aura of which, no five-stars can replace

It was 4 am when I heard the familiar sound of my flight commander's scooter outside my room. I was looking forward to another couple of hours snug in bed. That too on a Sunday, one day to chill after a hectic week of flying activity.

Squadron Leader Upadhya, or 'Uppy' sir, as we liked to call him was my flight commander. He ran all the operations of the unit. He could be heard from a mile away riding on his shrill sounding, dilapidated Vespa. And him coming so late at night, rather, early morning- could mean only one thing—there was a mission. He had come to 'detail' me the job. Putting on my dressing gown, I opened the door to peer out into the dark, only to be met by Uppy sir trying to find the switch to ring my door bell.

'Good morning! I am so glad that you are awake,' he said. 'I hope you have had a good night's rest?' Before I could think of a reply, he went on. 'There has been an accident ahead of Gangotri. Some mountaineers have been buried under an avalanche. You have to go. Your co-pilot is Bhads (Flight Lieutenant Bhadauria) and the aircraft is being made ready as we speak. I will do the ATC formalities for you. Reach the aircraft directly and take off at sunrise. It is going to be a long day of search and rescue.'

This was the umpteenth time that I had been asked to take to the skies before the sun. I didn't mind it; it was an exciting part of my job really. It did mean that I would not get my much-needed morning tea and Parle-G biscuits, one of the many things I loved and didn't want to let go of.

Anyhow, I was ready to take off at the decided hour. The sweet silence of the morning was broken by the whining engine and the slapping rotors. We were soon off, up and away, climbing due north with the sun lighting up the horizon on our right. Our brief was to reach Harsil, a quaint and tranquil one-horse town situated on the banks of the river Ganga. We were headed to the origin of this river in the Gangotri glacier for our mission.

I loved early morning flying. The cool and calm air always made the ride smooth. With the sun belting down heat on to the earth, the turbulence would soon start. That could make the best of stomachs churn, especially the empty stomachs that we flew on.

We landed at Harsil for refueling after a two-hour sortie. I jumped on to the ground, breathing in the crisp-cold morning air laced with smell of the pine at this 8000 odd feet helipad. There were no technicians here to handle the refueling and post flight inspection and all jobs were to be done by us two pilots. As I stretched my limbs and looked into the skies, my stomach rumbled indicating that it needed its fill of hot tea and a breakfast.

However, Harsil hadn't woken up yet. Hopefully, our

helicopter reverberating in the valley would have woken up some of the birds and locals by now. Since it was a civil mission, the army wasn't aware of our plan, otherwise, they would have been ready with tea for us. Tea and breakfast weren't just human necessities in our case, they were our fuel—the fuel, we as pilots, needed to climb the high-altitude terrain ahead of us; both physically and mentally. If I had to explain it in simple language, it is kind of like how one doesn't allow a guest set for long journey to leave on an empty stomach.

And here I was–about to perform an important rescue mission unfueled. This could be a hazardous decision. If my blood sugar went haywire as we reached closer to the rescue area, we would be doomed. Anyway, it seemed like there was nothing that could be done.

I was searching for something under the seat while the refueling from the barrel was in progress when I saw a packet wrapped in a silver foil which wasn't a part of the aircraft equipment. Under the co-pilot seat, we found a flask of tea. Wow! our flight commander had been so thoughtful. He had managed to get the aircrew cafeteria opened early in the morning and our cook had hastily packed some bread and spicy *bhurji* for us along with the sweet and now, not-so-hot tea.

We weren't complaining though. We, who moments ago, were making our peace with going without any breakfast at all. Warm, if not hot, tea would do gloriously.

I am tempted to give you some history on how pilots came to be well fed before taking on missions. There was no provision of any 'Aircrew Ration' in the old days. One doctor (he deserves a medal) conducted a study and opined that pilots needed to eat well before they took to the skies so that they remained alert in the cockpit. He pointed out that lack of food led to hypoglycemia which, simply put, meant that the blood sugar levels went low and led to many physiological problems including pilot fatigue which would not be in the best interests of safety.

Once rations were approved, it led to the birth of the Unit Cafeteria, also known as the Tea Club. Units managed to get full-fledged kitchens going—trained their lascars to become cooks and an officer was detailed to carry out the duties of the 'Officer-in-charge, Tea Club'. This was an important duty. It required him to ensure quality and the availability of food and beverages for the pilots—before and after their missions.

As one landed from a sortie and started the post flight formalities, there was a man with a tray of water, tea, *nimbu pani* and biscuits right at the door of the café as if welcoming us back from a safe flight. No matter how one saw it, it gave a feeling of home.

The unit cafeteria became a symbol of josh and morale of the unit. A lot of effort went in to make it as good as any café can get. It had plush seating and a dining area, lots of posters (some naughty ones too) and it became one of the most important places of the unit besides the briefing room. Over numerous cups of coffee, tea or lime water, bent over a game of chess or carom, it was common to see pilots discussing every possible topic under the sun. Often, the unofficial debriefs on sorties, emergencies and weather were also carried out in this friendly atmosphere. It was a place to unwind and chill, besides doing some ground work too.

Often, we would call the families over for a Sunday breakfast to the unit—a ritual which is still followed today. The café would churn out a variety of delicacies and everyone enjoyed the holiday and festive atmosphere. Children and ladies also sat in the cockpit, clicked photographs, and enjoyed the sumptuous meal prepared by our cooks in the cafeteria.

The rations that were authorised and scaled were enough to feed the pilots through the day. Cheese, chocolates, cornflakes, coffee, tea, bread, butter, jam and not to forget the tins of baked beans, fish and meat. All this and more was 'issued' to us in adequate quantities. With a little barter of the 'extras', we could get some items exchanged from the local market to augment these rations. The officer-in-charge was to put up the weekly plan on the notice board. This little slip of handwritten information was one that no one wanted to miss. The time spent at the unit café post the morning briefing was special and I still get nostalgic thinking of those times.

As time went by, cafeterias became more and more sophisticated and resembled the modern upmarket cafés of today. Any visitor to the squadron would get a taste of the morale (and the meals too!) and josh of the unit by soaking in the atmosphere of the unit café.

These days, fighter pilots are often required to carry

out long distance and long duration missions, sometimes for more than six to seven hours. Their meals have to be specially crafted and packed inside the cramped cockpit so that they can quench their hunger pangs during the sortie. A fair bit of research and experimentation goes into designing these meals—all done in-house at the unit cafeterias.

But it was not just the cooks who cooked. There were also some keen pilots who knew a thing or two about cooking and would try their hands at a few dishes. If their friends liked the results, the recipe would be handed down to the cooks and these dishes came to be named after their inventors in times to come.

One could write a book on the innovative meals prepared at our café. I can't go without writing about *Mittal bhujia* and *Lukhnawi omelet*. The legend goes that a pilot named Mittal had taught the cooks to prepare *egg bhujia (Egg Bhurji)* in his special way–with loads of Amul butter, the onions fried to a dark brown before the beaten egg with masalas was introduced into the pan. The egg coagulated but the cooking continued on high heat till such time that the dish resembled caramelised popcorns. The *Lukhnawi omelet* was a dish of single fried eggs with a topping of butter fried onions, tomatoes and green chilies. These delicacies along with their creators soon became famous and were served in almost all cafeterias of Air Force over time.

It would not be out of place to pay respect to the men behind the scenes who made sure that pilots went with their stomachs full for missions and came back safely. The cooks, the helpers and the men who helped procure rations—all worked hard to see that the credo of the IAF, 'People First, Mission Always' was followed in letter and spirit.

At Harsil that morning, we had successfully fueled ourselves as well as our machine and were soon off to the Gangotri glacier to look for the missing mountaineers. Their luck as well as ours was good. We managed to find them and pick them up to safety after a long search.

The credit for a large part of the success of that mission must go to Uppy sir and the aircrew cafeteria staff.

The Customary Cheers!

·······✦········

From the sparkling whites to the bubbly brews
Available are many potions for one to choose
Like the bar glasses of many shapes and sizes
Congruent are the men, who in throngs arrive
As the sun settles for slumber over the horizon
The pandemonium in the tavern begins to rise
A few bonds get nurtured, a few lost in strife
Such is the ambiance of the spirited confines

The dictionary describes the 'Bar' as a 'counter in a pub, restaurant, or café, across which drinks or refreshments are served'. Be that as it may, for us in the armed forces, the bar brings back so many people and stories and not so much the refreshments that were served across it. It takes me back in time to all the different bars at all the different officers' messes that I visited in my thirty-five years in uniform.

The wooden counters, the decorative silver and the paintings that adorned the walls, the bottles of different shapes and sizes with coloured spirits, the tall bar stools and the barmen. In every corner of the country (or outside for that matter) where a military establishment exists, a bar is sure to exist. Also called the 'watering hole,' the ubiquitous bar has many stories to tell.

****

'Anyone who tells me why a bar is called a bar will get two drinks on me,' said the Squadron doctor, Wing Commander S. We were in Chabua in Assam, as part of the military contingent which guarded our Eastern Borders. In this back of beyond, a 'trunk-call' could take hours or sometimes days to materialise and there was nowhere to go outside the camp area. So, the mantra our mentors passed on to us was—work hard, play hard and party hard—something that we followed religiously.

Our doctor was a bespectacled, well-built officer with a gigantic handlebar moustache and a smile to match. Very military-like in his mannerisms, he was very punctual especially when it came to getting to the bar in the evening. Exactly at 7.30 pm, the official bar opening time, our man would be at the door, well turned out in his mufti, smelling of old spice and hair oil.

He would sit down with his weight partially on the bar stool with his right leg on the floor. All he had to do was to make eye contact with the barman and the drink was in front of him in quick time—his usual-double large rum with a wee bit of water. As the drink was served, he would dip two fingers into the dark and slightly diluted spirit and sprinkle some drops around as if it were holy water! Dr S did not believe in sipping his drink. He would gulp down the dark brown liquid in three or four big swigs, swirling the fluid in his mouth under his big whiskers.

As it went down his hatch, he brought down the glass on the bar counter with a little thud, after which he ran his fingers over his handlebar moustache. In this interlude, the barman was expected to be ready with the refill.

A little later, at about 8, when we youngsters trooped into the bar, the old man would have taken out his pen and would be writing poetry on any piece of paper he found (paper napkin was his favourite), his fingers running through his hair, his palms caressing his face, Dr S in deep thought.

As soon as we had our glasses in our hands, we would say a loud 'Cheers!' in chorus. We knew what was to happen next and waited for the bombardment to commence. As if on cue, as we were getting our first sips, the poetry recitation would commence. Poetry was alien to most of us, but we all nodded and appreciated his efforts. This was a ritual that we didn't mind following; we had to keep ourselves in his good books, after all, it was he who would declare us fit for flying every morning.

In a while, the old man would finish his drink and narration, throw the paper away into the bin and disappear into the dark of the night, leaving us to ourselves.

In the old days, it was military custom for all to gather at the bar in the evening before dinner—whether you were a teetotaler or not, it didn't matter. Such traditions in the armed forces were so deeply ingrained in the system that I always thought that they would be difficult to be done away with. I distinctly remember that one of us was asked for a written explanation for not coming to the mess for dinner. But come the new era of gadgetry, some of these—especially the 'bar' traditions are seen to be dying.

Speaking of dying, in aviation, accidents happen and many good pilots leave us and go to heaven, leaving behind friends and memories. As a tradition, it was a done thing to gather at the bar after the final goodbyes were said and raise a toast to the departed. The accident would have dampened everyone's spirits, but this tradition at the bar helped everyone to get back to routine both in and out of the cockpit.

After a grueling week of flying our pants off, the weekend time at the bar was always an event to look forward to. We would finish our tasks a bit early on Friday afternoon and make a beeline for the bar to catch up on a beer or gin & lime. It was time to discuss the past and the future and vent our feelings. Bar rules were strictly followed. Whatever happened in the bar stayed in the confines of the bar.

Pilots, they say, never grow up. And in the times we flew, day in and day out, we carried our cockpit to the bar but never the bar to the cockpit. The debriefs of the sorties would continue albeit punctuated with humour brought about by the drink. And then there were a few who had legs waiting to be pulled to lighten moods.

Age, caste, sex, religion, faiths, beliefs, class—the bar was a place oblivious to all this. In the armed forces, we had a drink to socialise and not to get drunk as I had seen some of my friends in the civvy street do. We sat together, chatted up on every topic under the sun and strengthened our bonds of friendship—bonds that could never be broken for life. It was a place to unwind, to let one's hair down for a bit, to relax and rejuvenate.

Yet, there were some who could not remain sane and 'officer-like' after a few drinks, leading to a vitiated atmosphere. We were quick to escort them back to their rooms, reviving the decorum of the bar and of course, peace.

One of the most important pillars of this tradition was the barman. He was a part of the mess and was usually an old man—a teetotaler who was well respected by all. We heard fascinating stories of the bygone era from him and there was so much to learn from his anecdotes.

I once had the fortune of going to the mess which my father had frequented as a young officer. The barman–Bade Mia, still going strong–was happy to know of my lineage. As I ordered my whisky, he was quick to comment, 'Your father was a hardcore rum man. How come you have not taken to drinking rum?' I replied that I did have rum and other drinks once a while. He nodded his head in disapproval and began to recount stories of my father.

As the clock struck 9.30 pm, he picked up the small brass bell lying in the corner of the bar counter and jangled it with flourish indicating the closing time—something he had been doing for half a century. One was allowed to order a 'last' drink after this bell was sounded. As he closed shop, he said, 'Your father was a smart guy. He would order a last drink for all (even if they didn't want one) just before the bell was sounded!' He gurgled with laughter and continued, 'These days, not many come here. We have a full house only during official functions.' I noticed a glint of sadness in his eyes as he said that.

Barmen like Bade Mia were strict and were guardians

of the military traditions. Should you be improperly attired, he wouldn't serve you your drink and politely ask you to leave. He would also see to it that you did not have one too many in your exuberance and talking loudly was a strict no-no.

All of us army men, in and out of uniform (like me), reserve a small place at home in the drawing room to serve as a bar. Even when one can have a drink in pajamas at home, I for one, like to dress up as I did in 'those' times. Smartly attired, I walk up to the cubby hole to pick up my poison when the sun goes down. Over the years, in my travels all over the world, I have managed to pick up spirits of differing colours, strengths and taste. I love to see these bottles of different shapes standing tall, arranged military-like in my bar. They remind me of my journey in uniform and take me back in time, connecting me to the happy memories of golden times in my retired years.

The Queen Comes Calling

.... ✤ ....

Majestic grandeur
Unparalleled in radiance

Electric atmosphere
Imaginations taking flight

Tastefully decorated
Delicacies and environs

Disciplined demeanours
Defying hearts' flights

Precious memories
Etched unto eternity

We, the cadets of the 65th course of the National Defence Academy (NDA), were proud to see and interact with Queen Elizabeth on her first and only visit to the academy in our sixth term in 1983, of which we have vivid memories. A lot of hard work and toil was required on our part to make sure that the Queen went back suitably impressed with the future leadership of our armed forces.

While the administration did what they had to do to apply spit and polish and plan the visit to the T, we were told that it was essentially 'our show' and the Queen was specially coming to see us cadets.

As final termers, we were almost at the fag-end of our training, trying to enjoy the best part of our senior term and looking forward to our passing out parade at the end of the year, that, by the way, was to be reviewed by none other than the then Chief of Air Staff, Air Chief Marshal Dilbagh Singh.

The academy was, in true military style, bedecked for the occasion. Whatever was static had received a fresh coat of paint, flowers blossoming in pots lined the roads, flags fluttered all over the academy and barricades came up overnight.

The atmosphere was electric, and that is an understatement. Having no access to the TV and a non-existent social media, we cadets had only 'heard' of the royalty and seen pictures in print. To see her live at the celebratory functions planned in her honour along with Prince Philip, the Duke of Edinburgh, raised our excitement levels many a notch.

A grand parade was organised especially for the Royals, which was to be commanded by our course-mate Ravneesh Aujla aka 'Rocky', who incidentally stood first in the order of merit later. Post the parade, there was a ceremonial lunch planned in her honour, where the 1600-odd cadets and guests were to break bread together in true Brit style.

Whatever is done in the military is practised to perfection. The parade practice went on morning, noon and sometimes into late evenings till such time our adjutant was hoarse from shouting at us atop his horse. The horse and he would trot around the drill square moving between the multitude of rows and columns of boys in white patrol uniforms and see to it that no one shammed.

It was the first time a new 'technology' was being tried out on parade.

The 'white patrol' uniform sported a white cotton tunic with gleaming brass buttons and other accoutrements; with the trouser of the same material held down with an elastic band which went around the shining black boots. As the cadets were ordered a turn right or left, the flash of the shiny brass coming in and out of view of the audience was a mesmerising sight. Whilst this movement was done in one smooth motion in normal course, there was a need to modify it to be done in a slow, deliberate and coordinated manner so that the moment could be savoured.

A new timing for the turns was incorporated; and it took some doing to practice the new technique. During the turn, after one turned ninety degrees, the cadets were to freeze for a second or so, after which, in a swift moment, the boots were to come crashing down in unison–the metal undersides making a crunching sound on the tarmac. When 1600 of us stamped our feet together, what the audience heard was like a thunderous clap of thunder.

But there was another problem here, the sound of the boots had to reach the Queen at the same time. The parade was almost 600 meters long; the voice command by Aujla took some time to travel that far and therefore the reaction of the farthest squadron was delayed by a few microseconds making the manoeuvre look shabby. All the knowledge of physics and mathematics was applied so that the actions of all cadets appeared synchronised. When the experiment found success after a few hits and trials, we were finally in sync with each other and the new 'technology' became second nature.

Her Majesty arrived in a horse-drawn buggy to the tune of the trumpeters and was received on parade by the commandant, Rear Admiral RP Sawhney, dressed in Naval ceremonials.

And what a parade we presented to the royals! Everything, thank God, worked out beautifully well and the Majesty surely was impressed. Speaking on the occasion, she commented, 'I have never seen such a large parade being commanded with such precision just by a vocal word of command. I would like to import this technology to England.'

A small incident that occurred during the march-past is fresh in my memory. Our squadron was following the parade commander, Aujla, and I was in the front column right in the centre of my squadron following Aujla's footsteps. As we turned to march past the dais, Aujla's lanyard unhooked from his shirt pocket and the long cord swung along with his hands, not looking very nice. There was no way he could stop swinging his arms and marching smartly since he was in view of the Queen who he was to salute in a minute or two.

About 200 meters from the dais, our very own drill instructor, Subedar Lobhi Ram *saab* sprang out of the side gallery and marched smartly alongside Aujla, and, in a smart moment, made things right. Aujla didn't dither, he continued swishing his cane and marched forward. Our drill instructor had saved our parade an embarrassing moment.

At the end of the parade, we witnessed the Queen presenting mementoes to a few Victoria Cross (VC) winners. These were brought in smartly on parade by our own cadet table orderlies who did their act flawlessly. Prince Philip was thoroughly impressed with their drill and asked his ADC standing by his side to get some gifts to be given to the four boys carrying the table with the souvenirs. Some of these 'boys' who have since retired from service, still have preserved the pen set gifted by the Royals.

P R Singh, another course-mate, narrates a funny incident during the parade, 'I was carrying the championship banner and standing in front of our squadron. As the jeep carrying the Queen and the commandant went past inspecting the parade, I was supposed to lower the banner to salute Her Majesty. So mesmerised was I looking at her, that I forgot to do it, getting the dirtiest of looks from the commandant travelling standing behind her in the jeep.'

The amazing lunch. Sixteen hundred cadets waited behind their chairs at attention waiting for the royalty to arrive for the six course meal. There was pin drop silence inside, something we hadn't experienced for a while. As the Royals took their seats, on cue, all of us were expected to pull our chairs back and sit down at our tables.

The manoeuvre of dragging the chairs without any screeching sound from the wooden floor had been practised many times over and we had perfected this art of 'noiseless seating' by then.

The lunch started with Mulligatawny soup followed by baked fish, chicken in some snazzy sauce and finished off with the famous trifle pudding, coffee and chocolate. And yes, the band in attendance played a different tune with the change of each course. Such a formal meal, not many of us saw ever in our lives again. Eating had also been practised. We had a full dress rehearsal a few days before the main event. The then Minister of State for Defence came to review all the arrangements and was to eat with us. The famous suave and dashing horse rider 'Pickles' Sodhi, our Equitation officer, doubled up for the Prince whilst his gracious wife and superstar Nafisa Ali stood in for the Queen.

This meal turned out to be quite a disaster with the minister coming in very late; and our grumbling stomachs and parched throats made us fidgety behind the tables staring at the soup going cold. The minister was in no mood to eat, probably he didn't quite relish the western menu on offer; and went through the motions of the meal at a rapid pace.

By the time our first spoon of soup went down our parched throats, he closed his plate forcing us to do the same. I suppose he wasn't briefed to take it slow so that we could eat; and at the end of it all, we felt cheated and hungry. Thankfully, after he left, we were allowed to finish the left overs.

A funny incident happened during the lunch. The minister was grappling with his knife and fork trying to cut into the boneless roasted chicken. While doing so, the chicken decided to fly out of the plate much to the amusement of others sitting around him. But he was cool about it; without batting an eyelid, he quickly retrieved it from the table with his hands and devoured the piece licking his fingers clean after he did so. Maybe, chicken was the only thing on the menu that suited his taste buds!

We were the champion squadron and got to sit in the central lobby of the majestic mess from where we could see the Royals eating. Aujla, who sat next to the Queen narrates, 'I don't even remember eating a morsel that afternoon. The Queen saw that I was not comfortable and put me at ease with her charming banter. And she knew that the cadets needed time to eat to their hearts content and took her time closing her plate between courses. Something I am sure, was not needed to be briefed to her. She also asked me many questions about the training we were undergoing.'

Another trivia shared by Maj Gen Raj Sinha goes like this, 'We were to thump the tables when Her Majesty mentioned Lord Mountbatten in her speech. While we got used to the drill instructors saying the name during the practice in an 'Indianised' fashion–'Montbattin', we missed the same in the Queen's speech, and the mess didn't quite reverberate the way it should have with 1600 hands thumping the table in unison.'

The Queen and Prince, we were told later, were in India to celebrate their 36th wedding anniversary and were due to visit a church at Secunderabad after they left Pune. It was indeed one of the high points of our training at the National Defence Academy. More so, because the commandant was magnanimous enough to waive off all our punishment runs due to our contribution to the success of the event! As we went through our careers in the Indian Armed Forces, we always have had an anecdote or two to share about that morning of 21 November 1983.

The Queen and Prince died a year apart and are now united in heaven. What they have left behind for us are beautiful memories.

Man Friday

.... ✤ ....

Swiftly from the shadow he emerges
Fulfilling the daily needs and desires
As soon as everything gets organised
Back into the background he retires

A tower of strength, mate or buddy
To serve the senior he remains ready
From the uniform required for the day
Ready with machete, meals, or travel needs

At the beck and call of his commander
He remains as a devoted trusted aide
Meticulous in execution of all clambers
That all goes well, Man Friday ensures

Friday. When I was a young man in uniform, the word Friday meant a start of the weekend, a weekend which meant a visit to the bar, of socialising, of chilling, shopping and rejuvenating.

The other day, we were playing a word association game and this word cropped up. Someone mentioned 'Man Friday' and I am into rewind mode. The word, at least for me at that moment, is more associated with 'the man' rather than the 'day' it signifies.

My dad called this man his 'Man Friday' and we children grew up calling him *Bhaiya* (Big Brother). He tailed my dad through thick and thin, through peace and war and was part of his happiness and sorrows in his military life. In the British Raj, this man was called the 'orderly' (pronounced 'ordly' by us children), and the name stuck long after the Brits left us to ourselves. I also remember that this man was called 'Batman' or 'Batty' in short by some.

Why was the man called an 'Orderly' or 'Batman', I have oft wondered? Maybe, he was the one who got the *burra sahib's* life organised in an orderly fashion? Or maybe, he had the powers of 'Batman' from the comic strip, who would to do everything right and set things right. A bit of both, perhaps.

While dad was posted in the field, his Man Friday was everything for him. From waking him up in the morning with an enamel mug full of tea (he knew precisely the amount of sugar dad liked and how strong his *saab* liked his brew) to getting his uniform ready—the pips *brassoed* and shoes polished to a gleam, to ensuring that dad ate his meals and was comfortable in his bunker or tent, keeping his personal weapon clean and ready in its holster… you name it and he did it.

And he did it the way Dad liked it. He knew which radio station was to be tuned in to while dad shaved, he knew when to pour dad his drink in the evening and even see to it that he did not run out of his cigarettes. He would mend his clothes, get them washed and ironed and when dad was to go somewhere, he knew exactly what had to be packed for the journey. He knew the what, when, how and where of everything associated with dad's life. My mom jokingly referred to him as dad's 'first wife'.

I have known of so many of dad's friends who had these special men with them even after they both had done their stint in uniform. This Man Friday, orderly, batman, *bhaiya* and whatever name you gave him, was actually a trained soldier. A soldier who doubled up being an odd job man entrusted with the responsibility of looking after the likes of Daddy. This way, Daddy could concentrate on more important tasks of commandeering his men and keeping them battle ready.

To mummy's jibe at calling his man a 'wife,' he would reply, 'He does all that he does without as much as a whimper and he doesn't argue or fight with me ever. He is my most *wafadar dost* (loyal friend).'

And Dad, like so many of his friends that I can remember, took his man wherever he went on his official tour of duty. He even got his postings along with Dad and served him for most of his tenure in the army. When dad was away serving at the borders, he took his Man Friday along to his forward post on his long range patrols and on exercises in the middle of nowhere. During this tenure when Dad and *bhaiya* were away from us, we were lucky to get some help from the unit 'rear party'. This, another *bhaiya* was tasked to look after our basic requirements at home in the cantonments.

He was the odd job man for us. He came home in the morning, worked around the house repairing this and that, replaced a bulb, tended to a leaky tap, moved furniture, and also got us stuff from the market when needed.

With time, the British ways have faded and so has the concept of having an armed soldier for household help. And rightfully so, I think.

Dad was very particular and strict about the way his man was treated in the house. He was to be offered tea and a snack and never given any leftovers to eat. He wasn't allowed even to help us children with any of our chores. I remember, I did try once with very harsh consequences.

I asked 'Biru Singh', a six-foot gentle giant of a *Jat* from Haryana to put 'Blanco' on my PT shoes. Although *Bhaiya* did it happily for me, when dad came to know, he wasn't pleased at all. He then explained to us how such favours weren't 'authorised' for us and why he was officially allowed this *aide-de-camp*.

For us, *bhaiya* was a part of the family. He took us around on his cycle for joy-rides, made sure that Daddy's Lambretta scooter was always in working condition and clean and also helped ma sometimes in routine chores at home. He was around us when we did our homework, but unfortunately wasn't able to help us in doing it!

It was odd and difficult to understand for me at that time why *bhaiya* couldn't eat with us or sit on the chairs and sofas which were plentiful inside our home. He maintained respectful distance and treated everyone in the house with utmost reverence. I remember him, very hesitatingly, accepting something special made at home, and this too required a fair amount of coercion. Yes, a cup of tea was always happily had, but that too away from the eyes of the family, in some corner near the garage or behind the house where he smoked his *beedi* or gossiped with his other friends.

I always had a special attachment to my dad's *bhaiyas*. I would often trudge along with him at night, torch in hand, through the bushy path that led to the unit *langar* (cook house). Looking at the hardy *jawans* in awe as they ate their food, I would imagine myself like them in uniform. The attraction at the *langar* was to get to taste mutton in its watery gravy—cooked on wooden fire or the *Poori Chana and Halwa* (Spicy and Sweet delicacies) on Sundays. My mouth waters thinking of the food even now as I write this story.

Sometimes, it would be a walk through the unit

transport garages where I would spend time looking at the big and small trucks, daydream of driving them fast or get a look at the innards of an engine being repaired. Near the garages were the big Russian guns of the unit, parked immaculately in a line, with their barrels pointing into the sky and covered in tarpaulin. I got to touch their cold and smooth metal and move the barrels around with their control wheels when training of soldiers was in progress, of course, under his watchful eyes.

Everywhere I went, I met soldiers working at their stations, whom I bombarded with hundreds of questions. Being the Commanding Officer's son, I got attention, and the *bhav'* (pampering) was always in excess of what I actually deserved. And sometimes there was this secret rendezvous with *bhaiya* to the 'Wet Canteen' of the unit to have the forbidden tea and spicy samosa! He would also teach us to climb trees and use the *gulel* (slingshot) to get down the mangoes during the summers with some accurate shooting.

And then, there was 'Jose' who belonged to Kerala and was with us for many years till he retired. Jose uncle as I called him (he insisted that I call him that) taught me how to drive the jeep when my legs just about reached the pedals. He also took me home many a time, and his wife treated me with the tastiest *idli-sambar* and *dosa-chutney* that I have ever had in my life.

When *bhaiya* went on his well-earned leave, I would be in tears. I would start to miss him even before he left! To count the number of days left for him to come back, I would take out as many marbles as days left for him to return and put them in a tin. Every day, I would remove one marble and count how many were left. And invariably, when he got back, his bag would contain something for us from home. A wooden toy for me, some home-made sweets, pure ghee and pickles for the kitchen and much more.

Many years after my father retired, we had a surprise guest knocking at our door. An old and disheveled 'Mangilal Sharma' came down from 'Churu', a remote village of Rajasthan and found his way home in Pune. Sharma had been our cook for many years and had been with dad till he retired. How he managed to find his way home without a proper address is another story for another time.

In tears when he saw mom and dad, he first bent down to touch their feet. Having settled into retired life for many years, Sharma's children had moved out of their nests. Free of his responsibilities, the now old man decided to visit his *saab* one last time— 'Before my *josh* and *hosh* (enthusiasm and senses) leave me,' he said. He stayed with us for many days and insisted on taking over mummy's kitchen and feeding dad with the dishes that he used to like whilst in service.

With time come inevitable changes. The concept and ethos of the Man Friday of yesteryears has changed a great deal.

Be that as it may, I am sure there are several beautiful and inspiring stories of such men still untold. I salute them for what they did. Their dedication and devotion to the officers they served strengthened the might of our armed forces in more ways than one can imagine.

Home Away From Home

.... ✦ ....

Despite numerous hours spent ruling the air
There is always a lingering desire for the lair
Longing for laughter of family and friends
Sharing cordiality even in hardest of bends
For call of duty over the seas can we be flown
Meeting diverse people at places unknown
Always a bliss to find a warm affable smile
Altruistic and fearless even in terrain hostile
Bonds developed during such tough times
Ignite and suffuse the soul with joys sublime

Her hands held mine as we said goodbye. It was as if we had known each other for years. I could only hope that she had no other surprise planned for me; as such, I was already too indebted to her. I wasn't sure if I would ever be able to repay her kindness, warmth and love. I didn't know if I'd see her ever again, but I was leaving with something that would always stay entrenched in my heart.

April 2007, Kigali Airport, Rwanda.
The airport was bustling with people and energy. It was, after all, time for the only flight arriving from and returning to Nairobi. It was about midday, and, as usual, there was no news of the flight as we approached boarding time. Flights in this region of the Dark Continent seemed to operate on the whims and fancies of unknown forces. Despite the usual delays, we were confident that the flight would eventually arrive and take us to our destination sometime during the day.

I had made myself a convoluted plan for a holiday necessitated primarily because of lack of connectivity. Travel by jeep from Goma in the Democratic Republic of Congo to Kigali in Rwanda, catch a flight from Kigali to Nairobi by a local airline to collect my visa, stay the day at Nairobi and board a midnight flight to Mumbai.

At Mumbai, join my family at the airport and proceed to Australia and Singapore for a holiday.

The Indian Air Force had been kind to me. I had been deputed as a peacekeeper in the United Nations Peace Keeping Mission in the Democratic Republic of Congo 'DRC' (MONUC). Situated on the eastern border with Rwanda, was the quaint town of Goma from where my holiday was to start.

The cliché 'the back of beyond' suited this part of the world both, in letter and spirit. But soldiers don't mind staying in demanding field conditions. We almost enjoy it especially when we get to see and experience something new.

At Kigali Airport, I was contemplating where I would stay the night in Nairobi, when I ran into a young Indian guy in the waiting area. We soon got talking in Hindi and I promptly requested him to help me find a decent and safe place in Nairobi. He said he was in Nairobi on a business trip himself and didn't know places since he was to stay with a friend.

'Why don't you go and speak to that Indian lady in the white saree? She will surely be of help,' he said pointing to a group of ladies all clad in white sarees. He said he couldn't help me but he had, in fact, been of immense help as it would turn out.

Frankly, I am quite a babe in the woods outside the confines of a military camp. The confident gait and attitude—all vanishes the moment I step into *civvy* (civilian) street. The ladies were of many nationalities. One petite lady and her assistant appeared to be Indian and I decided to speak to them. I broke through their circle disturbing their animated conversation and managed to greet the Indian lady with a stuttering 'Goood AAfterrnooon!'

She was warm and forthcoming from the get-go. 'Are you Pakistani or Indian? What brings you to this part of the world?' And soon enough, I found myself at ease with this motherly figure. We walked a little away from the main group and continued our conversation. The ladies, I was told, were from the Brahma Kumari sect. The Indian lady—I will call her Lady L—told me that she was the head of their ashram at Nairobi. She also revealed that they were returning from Kigali after attending a conference on the 'Serve Africa' project.

We chatted about this and that but I still had not garnered the courage to ask her for help. Our chat was interrupted by the departure announcement of our flight. When she picked up her small bag and slung it over her shoulders, I mumbled, 'Ma'am, would you be able to help me with a place to stay in Nairobi?'

'Meet me after you clear immigration at Nairobi, let's see what we can do for you,' she said in Hindi. I was grateful for the little assurance and boarded my flight with a sense of relief.

Nairobi was a big mess of an airport, more like a bus stand packed with hordes of travellers. I realised why this was called the hub of Africa. Lady L surely had the right contacts in her hometown as I saw her group exiting immigration through a VIP counter while I was stuck in a 'normal' queue.

It appeared that she had forgotten me, as the group of Brahma Kumaris walked towards the exit. My heart skipped a beat as I saw my chance slipping away. And then, as if she had heard my mind, Lady L turned around, waved out to me and gestured to meet her outside. I felt a surge of confidence return. The kind lady then requested her security escort to help me clear the immigration faster and in no time I was at the exit, lugging my two big suitcases.

A sky-blue Impala, chauffeured by a man in whites awaited us under the porch. Squeezed in between the five ladies, we drove to the Lotus Temple, called The Raja Yoga Centre, in the heart of town. Behind the temple, I observed a large ashram compound with some living areas. An escort was called for, and I was ushered to a comfortable air-conditioned room which was to be my abode for the night.

The warmth of Lady L seemed to have permeated all over the estate. As I went around discovering the green and serene ashram campus, I only received warm smiles and welcome nods which made me feel like a Prince.

There appeared to be an overflow of positive energy everywhere. So far away from my military campus and my country amidst so many foreigners, in such a brief time this felt like home away from home. I was overwhelmed.

At dinner, I was greeted by fragrances of a typical Indian meal which was soon served in a large dining hall. Just a handful of people sat around me to eat an early dinner. Lady L stood behind me throughout the meal and ensured that I was served well. I gorged on an excellent hot Gujarati meal, which I quite enjoyed. I had eaten 'home' food after quite a while, something that I had been missing at our camp at Goma. I had truly eaten 'to my heart's content!'

Lady L asked me if I had any plans after dinner. I had thought I might see what a night club in town was like, since I had heard a lot about Nairobi's nightlife but I was too shy to tell her the truth. 'Nothing much,' I said. 'Maybe a stroll in the local markets.'

'No-No-No—NOOO...' she interjected in a shrill voice. 'You sure know the way to get lynched in Nairobi, don't you?'

'Please, please do not go out anywhere. Instead, attend the evening prayers with us and I will introduce you to the community here.' It seemed that my outing was a no–go now. I had no choice but to oblige her. I did not regret it though. I was to have an experience that I may not have ever had if I hadn't stumbled into this place.

The people at the prayers were mostly Indian, and I was proudly introduced as a 'Pilot from the IAF'. It was nice to see some of our own in the middle of Africa. These families had been here for generations and had learnt and absorbed the local culture, yet the Indianness hadn't gone out of them. I was also happy to learn that our countrymen had so much of a role to play in the development of this part of the world, hardly known to many in India.

The next morning, I had to go to the High Commission to get my visa stamped. I wasn't expecting royal treatment at this stage. But that was not to be. The Impala with an escort drove me to the commission. As I reached the reception, I was promptly ushered into the office of the Head of Passport section and offered a cup of tea while the paperwork was completed. I understood that my host had used the influence of her office to get my work done pronto. Since the job at hand was done sooner than expected, we had enough time before lunch to be taken for a tour of the city.

Nairobi was much like our towns—the traffic noise, hundreds of pedestrians walking hurriedly to and from work, children playing in the streets, right down to the piles of garbage.

Later in the evening, I packed my bags again after a shower and was soon on my way to the airport. I only realised after I reached the terminal that Lady L had ensured that I would go through immigration and depart like a VIP.

We meet so many people in the journey of our life and little do we know when and how these meetings blossom into friendships. I thanked my *karma* for the warmth and love of people I had never met in my life before and was soon on my way for my planned holiday.

After takeoff, as I peered outside the small window of my airplane looking at the city lights disappearing below, I joined my hands in gratitude to the wonderful people I had met in Nairobi. Lady L had reminded me that treating all who I come across with warmth and love meant something, even though our paths may cross for but a moment. I didn't know if I'd see her ever again, but I was leaving with something that would always stay entrenched in my heart.

Pottering On A Train

······· ❖ ·······

Seekers gain insights
From every journey undertaken

Worlds expand and evolve
By changes in place and perception

Living in the moment
Can be arduous, yet, fulfilling

Newer alliances brew up
Putting faith in impermanence

Destinations eventually arrive
With each lost to their grind

All journeys excite me. Trains especially. The rattle-tattle and humdrum of the wheels, swaying and shaking of the coach, the people and the scenery passing by…all this is super-romantic! And, if one finds good company, you can't ask for more.

I am travelling on the superfast Shatabdi Express to the National Capital. This is a short journey and God and Indian railways willing, we should be there in just three and a half hours.

I enter my compartment and make a bee-line to my seat 21. Thankfully it's a window, and whilst the country side whizzes by, I should be able to get some ideas for my next story.

Oh! There is someone already sitting there. An oldish couple, maybe one has come to drop the other…

I look at them and query in my best military manner. 'Excuse me sir, what would be your seat number? I am booked on 21 in this compartment.'

'Err, we are two of us and we have two aisle seats. Please sit there across!' He almost orders me, pointing in the direction.

No choice. I can't be un-military like now. Muttering under my breath about losing my window seat, I settle down for the journey. Fate accompli.

I look at the passenger next to me. It is a young lady double masked up, carrying a book but ready to sleep even before the train has moved. So that's that. No window, no one to speak to…this is going to be one boring three hours. Perhaps in the days of Covid, it is better to avoid conversation, I reassure myself.

I think of my journeys of the past where I have ended up making friends for life.

Rummaging through my backpack, I take out my little iPad. Sudoku, my downloaded books and of course–my Tintin and Asterix–are are all packed in here for my entertainment at the touch of my finger. I open up a game for a start, and so does the train with a lurch.

Shatabdi trains have recommenced serving meals on board thankfully. I see the soup arriving along the aisle as we chug out. My chicken meal will follow soon.

The soup sachet empties into a paper cup and hot water poured over it makes a decent tomato broth. Not bad. The lady besides me struggles with her pouch, which she can't seem to tear open. She looks at the silver foil in despair and then at me.

I am reminded of the pineapple tin and the *Three Men in a Boat*! The military man in me awakens. 'Ma'am, can I help you please?' I say, taking the packet from her. Thankfully, I can tear it open.

She laughs, is grateful, and her mask comes off.

Between sips of soup and crunching crispy soup sticks, the conversation is about to warm up. Perhaps, a hot soup is needed to start a chat on this cold and clammy day.

She isn't as young as I thought she was when I see her

sans the mask.

'What do you do for a living?' I ask for starters.

'Oh, I am a potter by profession and teach pottery to whoever wants to learn!'

'Wow! I haven't ever met a potter on a train!' 'I see that you like to read,' I say, tapping her book. 'Nice one this!'

Pointing towards the rear, she says, 'I was here for a cycling trip for a few days and now I am on my way back to Pondicherry where I live. What about you?'

'I live in this city for the time being...To which place do you belong? You don't look like a person from the South!'

'Actually, I am from Mumbai where I grew up and worked for about fifteen years, changing three to four jobs in the corporate sector. When I got sick of the fast and furious life, I decided to pursue my creative side, which has now become my profession.'

'Oh wow, Mumbai! Where in Mumbai do you live? I am a Punekar and have friends in Andheri, where I go often.'

'Small world this is! I too lived in Versova for most of my life before I migrated to Auroville.'

'Lovely place, Auroville. I have been there so many times!' I go on to describe my travels and travails in this beautiful township of Tamil Nadu.

'By the way, do you know a Frenchman by the name of Claude? He is an author of repute and an expert on Tibet and China and stays there...'

'Oh! of course I do. I was his neighbour for six

years. This is turning out to be a smaller world than I imagined!' she exclaims in glee.

The train trudges along and I decide to tell her a little about myself–how I became an author/writer after being a pilot for many years, all interesting stuff that I have done in my life, my family etc.

'Can I get to read something that you have written? I generally avoid Indian authors, by the way.'

I take out a copy of my book, *Up in the Sky*, and tell her about the short stories carried in it.

'Read this one about how I met someone on a bus in Africa. This meeting with you takes me back to an adventurous journey in this far-away land. Read it now if you want to!'

The lunch arrives and we talk about writing and reading over mouthfuls of railway food, which, by the way, is good now-a-days.

'I liked what you wrote about your African journey.'

'That's one Indian author under your belt then. Thank you.'

We shall soon be at our destination. It is time to say goodbye. I sign my book with a small note on the first page for her, 'Happy to have met you on yet another interesting journey of life! All the best for your future and hope to keep in touch.' I also put down my mobile number just below my signature.

'Thank you, thank you. You are most kind hearted and benevolent. I am so happy to receive a signed copy from the author!'

'That's nothing really. This book will remind you of our brief association! Your payback will be a review please!'

'Yes, I surely will. I will present this book to our library after reading, when I reach Pondicherry. Hopefully, more people will be able to read and appreciate your writing!'

'Thanks so much. Let me help you with your luggage!'

We alight from the train. She and I are going almost to the same area in Delhi. Maybe, we could pool a cab, and perhaps extend this little association a little longer. My mind plays games.

Nothing of that sort happens. We get into separate cabs outside the station and lose each other in the maze of city traffic.

It has been a sweet and short association with a potter on a train. Maybe, this experience can be my next story.

Meanwhile, I await a message to arrive from an unknown number...

Uff...Will She, Won't She?

.... ✣ ....

Impermanence whispers in the wind
Reminding us that all things end
Nothing lasts, everything must go
Like leaves that fall with autumn's blow

Short meetings, brief encounters
Moments shared with passing strangers
And we, mere twigs in the river's flow
Are swept away, where we don't know

News of death, reminds us of our fate
Echoing the fragility of our state
Stories kept inside, remain untold
Fading with memories, lost and old

Impermanence, a harsh but true friend
Teaches us to cherish what we tend
To live in the present and thrive
To embrace every moment of being alive

The flight was full. And so was the waiting area around the boarding gates at the newly constructed airport terminal at Mumbai. There was something about the two girls wandering around with small bags around their shoulders which caught my attention.

It was quite some time ago; I think sometime in 2001-02 but I remember it all.

They were well dressed, rather, 'nattily' dressed would be a better expression. And they certainly carried themselves and their dresses well like models do on a ramp. One was fair, her looks were quite like a girl who had descended from the hills. Pug nose, eyes that closed–almost–when she smiled, and a petite little figure to match. The other one was tall, dark with sharp features and black eyes that were as bright as coral. She must be from the South- Bangalore? Chennai? Hyderabad?? Somewhere there I guessed.

I thought she looked at me, and her smile broke into laughter. Oh...Aahh, it wasn't me who had generated the smile; she seemed to be looking *through* me rather than *at* me. Both the girls were chatting non-stop as only girls can, as they walked hand in hand across from where I was standing.

I have always been intrigued by the way Hercule Poirot and Sherlock Holmes go about analysing people and solving mysteries…and I often try and emulate them especially during my travels. I decided to indulge in this pastime with the two girls.

My mind went into assessment mode and I quickly commenced my analysis. What were the common features that linked the girls? Dressed well, confident walk, smile and an attitude that made me box them into the 'filmy' type. Bags–Gucci–from wealthy backgrounds, I surmised.

Were they on my flight to Delhi? Most probably. Had I, or hadn't I, seen at least one of them earlier somewhere? On a cover of a magazine maybe... Letting my thoughts be, I looked at the big screen for the flight time and boarding gate to be announced. And as soon as it was, a serpentine queue formed within no time and the quiet of the airport was broken by excited chatter of people wanting to board as soon as possible.

Why is everyone in a hurry to get on the flight? And on landing, they are most anxious to get off too…and this doesn't go down too well with me. It is not really my style. After all, I was an officer in the military, a Pilot at that, and waiting for my turn without any panic is the correct thing to do–officer-like, in my opinion. I decided to occupy the now empty seats in the waiting area to wait for the human serpent to empty itself into the aeroplane. The only niggle in my mind was if I would find a place for my carry-on bag in the overhead bin in the aircraft.

I was soon sitting by the window, watching the activities going on outside the aircraft. Refuelling was on, bags were crawling up the belt into the belly of the aircraft below me and the food truck attached itself to the starboard exit to load up all that it had for the hungry and thirsty passengers. An oldish-looking gentleman, very military-like in a tie and jacket, plonked himself on the aisle seat, giving me a nod and a smile.

I wondered where those girls were seated, as I strapped myself to the aeroplane. Looking up, I noticed them walking down the aisle. The dark one took her seat a few rows ahead from where I sat while the mountain girl walked further up dragging her strolley, looking for hers. I looked on my right at the empty seat and looked at her and again at my seat...

Will she? Won't she?

And then, there she was, a few moments later, asking to be allowed into the seat next to mine. Maybe, I was in for some good conversation and an interesting flight ahead.

'Hi!' I said as she sat down with a sigh. The old man across gave me a quizzical look, as if asking me if I knew the lady. We were soon on our way, taxying to the beginning of the runway for take-off. The first officer from the flight deck announced that there would be some delay before we actually took off due to traffic congestion. Again a queue, I mused. Might as well pick up conversation before the engines roared to life, I thought.

I told her my name. I am on my way to Delhi for a day for some work. 'Do you live in Mumbai or Delhi?' I shot her the obvious opening remarks.

'Here only,' she replied. 'I am going to Delhi with my friend for a shoot,' said she. 'Shoot what?' I asked quizzically, sounding foolish. 'An ad film,' she said smiling her pearly whites at me. 'What do *you* do?'

Ahh!!...wasn't I waiting for that question! 'I am a helicopter ***Pilot*** (with emphasis on **Pilot**) in the IAF,' I answered. You see that hanger on the other side of the runway? Well, that is where my office is and that is where I fly my helicopters from.'

The word 'Pilot' always and every time has evoked a 'wow' and surprised reaction from all strangers I have met on buses, trains and planes and wherever else. Their faces light up, they are happy to be in elite company of someone who can 'fly' and they always have some basic questions to ask. Being put on a pedestal by hitherto unknown co-travellers surely would give anyone a high!

The reaction this time was no different. The old man in the seat gave me another stare and I tried to keep him out of my sights.

Amidst the din of the engines at full power during take-off, I was explaining the principles of the aerodynamics of flight to the now fully interested listener. The old man continued staring at me while I continued trying to ignore him as best as I could. It was getting weird; was he plain jealous that I was hogging the limelight or did he want to contribute to the conversation?

Oh! The myriad range of topics that we spoke about that morning. The conversation continued through breakfast and very soon, we were like long lost friends talking of this, that and the other. We compared how stressful life was in the different worlds that we lived in and how all of us were coping with the changed life in this fast-changing world. We exhausted politics, religion, technology, foreign policy, human relations and more in the 90 odd minutes at 36,000 feet. I could write an essay on life in tinsel town now; having been given some first-hand knowledge of the film industry.

The plane had commenced descent and the passengers were getting fidgety already. If we had a way of getting off then and there, I think some of them would have chosen to jump out to land in their backyards in the suburbs they lived in. It was time to wind up our conversation too and exchange phone numbers. 'Come over to my squadron someday to see the helicopters! I invited her, handing over my card. 'Yes, of course! Would love to see the machines up close!' she said as we touched down.

The man in the third seat was still fidgety, I noticed. Perhaps I should give him a chance at conversation, I thought.

'Sir, do you live in Mumbai?' 'Yes,' he smiled for the second time since he allowed me into my seat. 'Work or leisure trip to Delhi?' I continued. 'My daughter stays here and I am going to spend some time with my grandchildren for a few days,' he answered, his eyes lighting up.

'So, you are a helicopter pilot in the IAF?'

'Yes sir!' I replied intrigued by his interest in my profession.

'When were you trained at the HTS (Helicopter Training School)?' The use of the acronym had my tentacles along with the hair on my head standing up. This man sure had something to do with my profession.

'1984', I replied.

'Who was your Commanding Officer then?' I thought for a second... and then it dawned on me–this is one time I wished there was an escape hatch in the floor below me from where I could deplane and escape.

I was face to face with my Commanding Officer of almost 20 years ago.

It was a sheepish and ashamed me who spoke, 'A thousand apologies sir, I should have recognised you.' I felt like pulling out the life jacket from under my seat and becoming an ostrich for the rest of my time at the airport.

As we de-boarded the flight and went to the carousal to collect our bags, my new found friend asked me how I knew the old man.

'Oh, the IAF is a small place and we generally know each other,' I said, looking to see if the old man was anywhere in earshot.

I didn't want to run into him for a few years from now. Thankfully, he hadn't corrected my aerodynamics and the other *gyaan* about flying that I was imparting to the young model.

We said our byes and the experience with the *Page-*

3 girl and my ex-boss went into the background. I had managed to get an autograph of the model which I would present to my little daughter.

I was soon back in Mumbai and wanted to recount my experience to my family at the breakfast table on Sunday. The little slip of paper which I wanted to gift my daughter was to be given after I told them the story.

The Sunday edition of the newspaper lay in front of me as I called them all around me. As I waited to start the narration, I turned the page-3 glancing through the headlines and photographs.

A photo stared at me. The small script under it read, ... the upcoming model and actress found dead at her home in Bandra'. The police investigating had commented that it was, in all probability, a case of suicide.

I stared at the photo and re-read the news.

It was my friend on the flight.

My story died inside me...

'Lost' Stories

•••••• ✤ ••••••

*Adversity and joy operate in an osmotic
relationship
Diminishing of one makes the other to diminish
Narrowly separated by a degree of torment
Each act as a conduit to fearlessness
Having lost is not always a failure
Winning is not a success always
Each of these can occur in concurrence
Down and out is a perspective not a verdict
Just a recluse for whose lips are oiled with excuses
Adding wretchedness to who in mind are
vanquished*

Two young pilots in the aircrew room. All incidents narrated are true. Names have been changed to protect identities.

Flight Cadet Andy: Hi Pat, what's up? No sortie for me today. My instructor is on a short leave!

Flight Cadet Pat: Hey! Andy, me too! I am off flying programme. Feeling a bit lost—to be away from the cockpit.

Andy: Am feeling lost too. What to do, man? Let's watch some stuff on the telly or play some chess?

Pat: The old man may saunter across and give us some file work to do. Let's just keep a checklist in hand and gossip.

Andy: Let's do that!

Pat: Speaking of lost, yesterday, there was such bad weather. I was on my first navigation sortie with my instructor. I couldn't see a fig on ground and just carried on fighting with my map and DR (Dead Reckoning). As I kept trying to find where on earth we were, my instructor lost it when I told him I had no clue where we were!

Do you want to know what he did?

Andy: Tell me.

Pat: I tell you, it is a crazy story. He dived to low level and we flew inverted! If this was not enough, while doing so, he wanted me to see the features on the ground and co-relate the position on my map. How can one do that with the blood rushing to the head and the map flying around in the cockpit, *yaar*! I was scared to even think clearly and gave up, telling him that I was lost. The expletives that he threw at me! We abandoned mission. He warned me that if I didn't improve my sortie preparation the next time, I shall be forever 'lost' from flying. Poor joke. Only he laughed at it.

Andy: I am sure he would have been lost himself when he was learning how to fly. Never mind, better luck next time! Let me return the favour and tell you a story.

Pat: Sure. Go ahead!

Andy: Our course mate Ramu, who flies helicopters, told me a story when he called me up this morning. He was going from Hyderabad to Bidar and got lost on the way with his instructor. His instructor descended the helicopter to tree top heights and followed a railway line to a station where he hovered—asking Ramu to note the name on the platform and co-relate it on the map. Cool *na*? These helicopters can't get lost; don't you think? I am told that they have landed in fields and asked people for directions!

Pat: You are right. I just read in the flight safety magazine the other day. There was this helicopter going from somewhere to Jodhpur. They got lost and by the time they managed to find their position in the desert, they had run out of fuel!

Andy: Then what happened? Is it a recent incident?

Pat: Oh, that is an interesting tale. They landed on

a road close to Jodhpur and blocked the road—causing quite a jam and headline news! With police help, they rang up their flight commander to tell him what had happened. Soon, a fuel bowser was sent to the site to refuel the machine. It must have been quite a sight for the onlookers!

Finally, when they got back to base, they were promptly grounded! It must have happened long ago. It was in that 'I learnt from that' section of the magazine. In those times, one had to fly with the thumb on the map and eye on the compass all the time—not like today, where we have such modern navigation equipment like the GPS to help us. Once we graduate from here on to newer aircraft, we would have all the gizmos to tell us where exactly we are, all the time. And then there will be no question of being lost, isn't it?

Andy: Don't you know of the famous story of the MiG-27? It got lost on a long cross country and almost ran out of fuel!

Pat: I heard about it but don't know the details. What do you know of it?

Andy: My instructor is a MiG 27 pilot and he told us of a story that happened in the '90s. There was this guy who was supposed to ferry one MiG-27 from Jodhpur to a base in the Northeast. It required him to carry a lot of maps on board since the route was so long. You know what he did?? After he marked his route on his maps, he smartly cut off a strip just about two inches on either side of the route drawn and wrapped this ribbon of a map around two pencils. As he kept flying towards the northeast, he just had to unroll his small map! It was a cool invention, and may be, the first of the 'moving map displays' that we have today! Why he did this is anyone's guess, but luck didn't favour him on that day...

Pat: Now you are getting to the good part. How did he manage?

Andy: Well, something went wrong with his compass and he veered course well to the south of the intended path. He was soon flying in circles somewhere near Lucknow trying to establish his position.

Pat: He had so many systems on board. Why didn't he use them? More importantly, why didn't he radio for help?

Andy: Men will be men after all, whether on ground or in the air! We don't like to ask for directions, do we?

Anyway, our man didn't want to tell the world that he was lost. And soon, some more of his navigation instruments started giving erratic readings due to bad weather. And to top it all, the radar in that area was switched off due to thundery conditions. So, effectively, he wasn't on anyone's radar scope either! You see, when Murphy strikes, he does so with all guns blazing.

Pat: Damn! Then what happened boss?

Andy: You know the way the MiG guzzles fuel—he soon realised that he was critical on fuel, and in desperation, he started giving blind radio calls. An alert controller at Bareilly heard him and then vectored him in for a safe landing. His engine almost ran dry that day, I am told.

Pat: He must have been fried, baked and roasted over coals for a long time. There are so many things to learn from such an incident. We must never be complacent... ever! The day you take the aircraft for granted, it takes you for a jolly good ride!

Andy: Absolutely! All these stories have something to learn from.

Pat: Then, there was this cadet who went for his navigation solo a few years back. He got lost and ended up South of Hyderabad. With no fuel, he had no choice but to eject out of a perfectly good airplane. Thankfully, he lived to tell his story. There have been so many who have disappeared from the face of this earth, you know. In this business of flying, there are no second takes, and if you try one, you have to pay with your life.

Andy: You are right. Some of our 'lost' pilots have sometimes even gone into enemy airspace due to a navigation error. Thankfully, they weren't shot at. That reminds me of another story which my instructor narrated.

Pat: We might lose ourselves in this maze of 'lost' stories soon. Let this be the last one.

Andy: The last one. For now...

So, there were these two senior pilots flying the Mi-17 helicopter in the Mizoram sector long ago. Both knew the area by heart having operated there for eons. But a stupid navigation error on part of the pilots led to an embarrassing situation. These guys were flying to a helipad to pick up a VIP. The weather was good and they were enjoying their trip. The calculated line on the map showed a flying time of 30 minutes to the helipad where they were supposed to pick up this senior officer. At 30 minutes, they reached a helipad and went in for landing.

As they settled the machine on ground, they realised something amiss. The guys who came to receive them were in funny looking uniforms and not Indian, as was everything else at the army camp teeming with activity.

They had landed in Burma. Once they realised their mistake, they quickly exited the area before any of the Burmese soldiers could reach the helicopter to find out if they needed any help!

Pat: Oops. That could have led to a very embarrassing diplomatic situation. What had gone wrong?

Andy: The fact that they crossed the border meant that a lot of things must have gone wrong! The pilots did not report their mistake on getting back and the Burmese authorities were kind too. They also let it pass as a case of lost pilots!

Pat: All's well that doesn't end in the 'well'!

Andy: Cheers to the pilots of the bygone era!

Cats Have Nine Lives. And Pilots?

.... ✥ ....

Life of a copter pilot is full of adventure
To terrains, unkind and easy, we venture
There's no scope to feed the head's blenders
All attention is diverted on cockpit's sensors
At times we test our luck beyond the limits
To our machine we transfer our rising spirits
In unison we conquer each and every obstacle
Even accomplish missions that seem a miracle
We journey together in every hue of the sky
Trusting our magic wings, together we fly
On our mental agility and resilience we rely

1987, Military Hospital, Dinjan... Eastern Assam. The far east.

Their faces looked like chicken roasted pink over coals, and, as I bent to hug them, I could smell the burns too. The fire had erased Bittu Sir's moustache, eyebrows and eyelashes completely and crumpled his hair into small curls.

In the bed next to his, was my dear friend GRS, who we lovingly called 'Grass'. He had a few scratches and burns but no broken bones.

They looked as if they had stepped out of a comic strip, and as I wished them 'Happy Birthday' rather loudly, they broke into laughter. Many of our IAF clan was there to meet them which led to the usually silent ward filling up with cackles and peals of laughter. Someone remarked rather loudly, 'Let us put some rum into the bottle of saline so that the drip can be put to good use!' The nurse on duty was not amused at all. She made a mental note to tell the doctor on duty about it.

Both Bittu Sir and Grass were upbeat. Even after having gone through what they had, they were joining in the banter and enjoying the attention. Both were endowed with a terrific sense of humour and had the ability to turn a serious situation on its head.

'Let us hear the story of what happened from the horse's mouth,' said one of the guys. The two horses were rearing to go, eager to tell us all.

'Yes, let's!' we all said in unison. All of us knew bits of information about the freak accident but wanted to know the juicy details. As such, since all had ended well, it would be forgotten in a few days as we went on with our lives in the sky.

'You see, Grass and I had gone for an instrument flying sortie. On the way back, we decided to fly a bad weather circuit and land with a curved approach. I was at the controls since Grass had done all the flying for the past 35-40 minutes and I wanted to show him the landing, as we would do in case we had to land in bad weather. Grass was enjoying the scenery around since he hadn't looked outside the cockpit for most of the sortie!'

'We did everything right and were curving in to land on the runway when the baby decided to fall out of my hands. She just bucked and ducked too low and then things went horribly wrong. I can still see the whole situation unfolding in front of my eyes,' said Bittu Sir as he closed his eyes sans the brows and lashes.

There was a pregnant silence which was broken by Grass who took over the narration.

'We were not aligned to the runway, and as we neared the touch down point, our left wing was almost touching the soft ground. Bittu Sir tried to get her straight but our left wheel touched soft earth and was sheared away instantly. The aircraft veered to the left and amidst the screech and groan of metal over concrete, we seemed to have lost our drop tanks (additional fuel tanks carried under the wing) as well as our other wheels. We were now heading straight for the blast pen on our belly.'

'Is it a pen which blasts? And how come you were on your bellies?' interjected one of the ladies, not familiar with flying jargon.

'Oh! Sorry. The blast pen is this concrete structure right next to the runway where we park our aircraft for readiness during war. It is basically a three-sided wall that saves the aircraft from splinter damage during enemy bombing. It has a simple wire mesh, over which vegetation is allowed to grow so as to camouflage it from above.'

The lady nodded and Grass continued, 'The solid wall was approaching us at full speed and soon we would be pulp. In panic, I pulled the ejection handle to escape from the aircraft. Thereafter, what happened is a blur,' confessed Grass. Fighter aircraft have ejection seats to help pilots to safely extricate themselves from a sick aircraft. When the firing handle is pulled, the seat is 'fired' out of the aircraft and subsequently, the parachute deploys letting the pilot float down to safety.

Bittu Sir was, at the time, one of the senior pilots of IAFs only formation aerobatics team—The Thunderbolts—that flew the Hawker Hunter aircraft. Grass was one of the youngest pilots of the team. As such, the Hawker Hunter that the two were flying was old enough to become an artifact in museums and amusement parks. Being on the last leg of its life, the oft quoted joke about the squadron went thus. 'What will happen if we take out the thunder from the thunderbolts? Obviously... only nuts and bolts!'

Bittu Sir, who seemed to have gone into deep thought for a while, continued the commentary.

'The next thing I realised was that the aircraft was screaming in pain as its belly scraped the tarmac, the momentum trying to make it climb the steep embankment of the wall. As we did so, the right wing of the aircraft met its end trying to cut through a pole which held the wire mesh of the pen. It was then, that my bad luck turned good—for reasons beyond my comprehension, the cockpit of the aircraft separated from the main body and got caught in the wire mesh. The rest of the aircraft carried on—on its final journey to destruction across the blast pen, bursting into flames.'

'Really! Absurd! Unbelievable! Only the cockpit separated and stayed behind with you both inside?' asked one of the young pilots, his mouth agape in astonishment.

Grass took up the baton. 'Only Bittu Sir was inside the cockpit. I had one hell of a journey after I pulled the handle,' he said with his cherubic smile.

'The seat mechanism fired and my seat with me strapped into it was almost out of the aircraft when we jolted with the impact with the pole. Maybe, due to this, the seat fell away, and the charge burnt without being able to propel it upwards. The drogue parachute came out of its housing and caught fire before it fell on my face. I felt I was dead and travelling in a white tunnel to heaven. Or hell maybe. I was back to my senses as the heat of the burning material started eating away my facial skin. Realising that I was alive, I threw the burning cloth away and got up to run away down the embankment to safety. Thanks to the fire-treatment, I think I have become a *gora* now,' concluded Grass with a laugh.

All eyes were now on Bittu Sir for the climactic moment of his story.

'Grass here is not telling how he kept his wits about himself and rescued me', started Bittu Sir. 'He saw that I was stuck inside the cockpit, completely dazed and in shock. I had had a more severe heat treatment than Grass, and I could barely see. Grass came to the cockpit and helped remove the straps and buckles that fastened me to the aircraft. I don't know from where he garnered the energy to pull me out of the mess, and to safety.'

'It is so sad that your parachute got burnt Grass. You would have had a memento of something that saved your life!' someone quipped.

Grass said, 'Oh really! If I had gone up with the seat, I wouldn't have gained enough height for the parachute to deploy and I would have ended up as pulp. You would have had to lift me up with a straw or a spoon. My bad luck turned good with the ejection system not doing its work!'

God makes his own rules. In the profession of flying, we often talk of Murphy's law, 'Anything that can go wrong, will go wrong.'

But sometimes some things that go wrong become thankfully right, and like Bittu Sir and Grass, you get to beat Murphy!

Dust To Dust

.... ✣ ....

Death is the only unchangeable constant
Unifying with dust is eventual covenant

Gifted are those who value each moment
Treating every breath as precious present

Few are bestowed the skill to understand
Perspective differentiates gold from sand

Some see stars as diamonds in the night
Some see only expulsions of fire and light

Optimists receive each sunrise with belief
Sorrowers relentlessly vent out their grief

Realisation of vulnerability dawns too late
The only option then is to succumb to fate

Those who can reflect on life with pride
Recognise, it is with earth we finally unite

'We have been born on this earth and have to go back into it one day. Why do we have to fight and argue over things that will not mean a thing after a while?' The tall, lanky, six foot plus Khalsa who I had always seen cool and calm was agitated this evening.

'Just chill man,' I said to my dear friend.

MSB and I were standing in the lawns of our mess bathed in the cool glow of a full moon. MSB who towered a good foot above me, was still fuming, red in his face and muttering to himself. We had just exited the dining hall after dinner, where an argument between a few—MSB included, had turned a tad ugly.

These were early days in the flying academy and we, barely out of our teens, were busy learning to aviate and survive the rigors of training to be pilots in the Indian Air Force. Life was tough and such nasty incidents didn't help at all.

The discussion had started off well with aviation related topics and flying concepts but some leg pulling by a few had transformed the scene into a mud-slinging match. Acidic words with references to our very origin– the Earth–were exchanged as things went awry. The group had to be dispersed to their rooms for the night.

The incident had not gone down well with MSB. As a friend, I felt it was my duty to placate him before we called it a night. I got him into a conversation about our past, families, crush on, and what we would be doing in a few years from now. This brought down the mercury.

'Oh! I must really be going now, I have an early morning solo and I need to prepare for it,' said MSB, pulling at the thin wisps of hair on his chin which would soon be called a beard.

'Yes, now that you are cool about things, yes, let's hit the sack.'

'Happy landings! All the best for tomorrow's sortie!'

The next morning, while waiting in the crew room for our sorties, we heard the wail of the crash siren from the Air Traffic Control. All of us trooped out into the early morning sun and looked skywards. There was no sign of any aircraft. Maybe, it was a simulated exercise we conjectured.

An instructor appeared from the duty room and herded us into the briefing room.

'MSB's aircraft has just crashed after takeoff. It doesn't seem that he had the time to pull the ejection handle. But let's hope for the best. No more flying for the day, you guys just stay in and study your notes and brush up on emergency procedures,' he said and walked away.

As we looked into the direction of takeoff, we could see some black smoke billowing from the ground a few kilometres away. We just hoped that our mate MSB would have survived the crash somehow, and waited for more news to filter in.

MSB died in the crash. His engine had failed as he climbed a few hundred meters above the earth. He would have had no time to think and pull the handle to bail out. He went down with the aircraft maneuvering away from the populated area to avoid collateral damage.

That night when I went into bed thinking of my friend, I visualised what he must have been through. With the engine becoming suddenly silent, the airspeed would have washed off within a fraction of a second, the aircraft would have started its downward descent soon thereafter. In a matter of seconds, what had been built out of the earth would have vaporised into earthy material again.

MSB had surely saved many lives by veering the aircraft away from the populated area in the few seconds of reaction time he had. They say, as one approaches death, the entire reel of life flashes by in front of your eyes.

And, if what they say is true, MSB would have thought of his school, parents, friends, and girls in the few seconds he had in the air. Just before impact, maybe, he also thought of our chat from the night before.

Rest in Peace, MSB.

Unforgiving Omission

.... ✣ ....

*Suspended
in the hammock
of time and space
Floating
in the twilight
of unconsciousness
Triumph and tragedy
of enhanced ambiguity
Ruminating on possibly
unanswerable queries
Obscurity
expanding tentacles
around reality
Flawing inevitably
human perceptivity
Unknown
to the power
that coerced inaction
Emerging as a target
of infinite contradiction*

Currency notes clung on the half-broken tree fluttering in the breeze, tattered aircraft parts lay strewn all over the woods and a strong stench of kerosene filled the air. A few more trees had been knocked over and lay in the deep furrow formed by the big aircraft when it impacted the ground. As one looked closer, some bones and charred flesh along with shreds of the blue flying overalls lay scattered, mixed with the debris. The young pilot was definitely dead.

We had taken off from Mumbai in our Mi-8 helicopter for the search and rescue mission after this fighter aircraft was declared 'missing' by Air Traffic Control. The search for the airplane was to commence around the place it was last identified on the radar and it took us close to Goa. That day, the low hills of the Western Ghats were shrouded in clouds and rain. With some difficulty, we reached the place of the crash and were able to identify the site due to the contrasting brown gash created in between the lush green of the forest.

While we hovered above to find a suitable place to land near the crash site, we saw people from the nearby villages crowding around the crater. Some children were trying to climb the tree to retrieve the currency while others searched around in the debris for more.

We realised that there was no one left to be searched

for, or rescued–this aircraft had just one pilot. What was left for us to do was to look for the 'black box' and 'cockpit voice recorder' along with some pieces of evidence required immediately for the inquiry. The rest of the aircraft or the bits left of it, would be picked up by the ground party arriving from Goa with special tools and equipment.

It was a sad end to the supersonic fighter's long and easy flight from one of the forward airfields in Punjab to Ozhar near Nashik in Maharashtra. Located at Ozhar, was the Hindustan Aeronautics Limited (HAL) facility created to overhaul the Russian made MiG-29. In a few months, this aircraft would have completed its entire make over, and would have been handed over back to the IAF to guard the skies of our country again.

A young and dashing Flying Officer was tasked to undertake this mission and had prepared well for it. He had just become operational on the aircraft and this was his first long ferry mission. He had spent a lot of time marking his map, memorising the route and readying himself for the long flight. Thereafter, he was briefed by his supervisors at the squadron for the mission.

An early morning takeoff was planned, so that the pilot could hand over the aircraft, catch a taxi to Mumbai and be on the last flight to Delhi. He carried just a pair of jeans, a couple of tee shirts and some toiletries wrapped in a towel. The ground crew had put his bundle inside a tiny compartment behind the cockpit. He also carried adequate money required for his return journey in the large pocket of his overalls.

All set for the mission, he would have walked to the aircraft, carrying his maps and helmet, and of course his oxygen mask.

To stay alive inside a fighter cockpit, pilots have to breathe oxygen provided by a special system which gets connected to this mask. At altitude, any deprivation of this life-giving gas would kill the pilot almost instantly.

The weather was fine and the aircraft ready for an on-time takeoff. But our dear old 'Murphy' was lurking around. As the pilot reached the takeoff point, the young man realised that the oxygen pressure had depleted and would be insufficient for the long flight. He returned to the parking bay and informed the technicians about the problem. Waiting in the crew room with a cup of coffee in hand, he saw the techies working on the ailment of his aircraft.

A leaky valve in the cockpit was the culprit. Since no spares were available at the unit at that time, everyone put their minds together to find a way out. A brilliant idea ensued and discussed threadbare. Since there was no other way out, it was decided to implement the same.

The idea was simple. The pilot was briefed to keep the valve closed till the aircraft took off and climbed above 10,000 feet since one could breathe normally up to this altitude. At this height, the pilot was to manually start the oxygen flow by operating the valve and use it for the rest of the mission which was to be flown at 40,000 feet. This way, a fair amount of oxygen could be saved from leaking.

Pressure to fly the mission was mounting from all quarters and it forced the supervisors to take the decision they did. The young pilot was OK with the idea and being briefed by his seniors, he was soon up and away into the blue skies in what was to be the last sortie of his life.

For reasons incomprehensible, the young man simply forgot to turn the valve 'on' during the climb. The aircraft climbed to its cruising altitude on autopilot, and navigated itself towards its destination. The effects of lack of oxygen must have started soon after the aircraft climbed beyond 10,000 feet and thereafter, and the poor guy would have slipped into slumber never to wake up from it.

The 'pilotless' aircraft flew along on its planned route aided by its own systems. Reaching overhead Ozhar, it carried on further—there being no inputs from the pilot. When the engines died due to fuel starvation, the aircraft would have stalled and plummeted to the ground.

A single mistake of forgetting to open a valve had led to the loss of the man and machine. His dreams and future disintegrated with the aircraft as it crashed into the jungle.

But I, for one think that the pilot should not be held to blame in totality. All the people in the chain which gave this mission a 'go' had a role to play in this loss. Technicians, senior pilots, supervisors and safety experts out there should have thought what all could go wrong if the idea was implemented.

Maybe.... maybe if, the pilot had switched on the

valve, the accident wouldn't have happened but I am sure that the oversight by every person in chain would have resulted in another one at another time.

The effect of forgetting something in life on terra-firma can be rectified, but in the air, it is a different story.

As I end this piece, I am reminded of a quote by an anonymous writer which is popular within the pilot community:

> *Whenever we talk about a pilot who has been killed in a flying accident, we should all keep one thing in mind. He called upon the sum of all his knowledge and made a judgment. He believed in it so strongly that he knowingly bet his life on it. That his judgment was faulty was a tragedy, not stupidity. Every inspector, supervisor, and contemporary who ever spoke to him had an opportunity to influence his judgment, and so—a little of all of us goes with every pilot we lose.*

Gestures Of Gratitude

········ ✤ ········

Anxiously scrutinising all rescue operations
Ruminating over findings of failed missions

Summoning courage for acceptance of reality
Chronicling my journey to its possible veracity

Aligning sockets to decipher every probability
Chronic discomfort with hovering uncertainty

Illusionary solace in pretentious declarations
Challenging channelisation of suppositions

Rationale failing to offer explanation of existence
Surrendering cognition to the divine influence

The entire Mehta family including the little ones and some friends were gathered together at Dr Mehta's residence, the senior-most member of the family. They had been invited over for a special occasion to celebrate the life of their son, Dr Minoo Mehta, a renowned doctor and mountaineer.

The family and friends waited to be introduced to the pilots who had taken part in the search and rescue of Minoo from the high reaches of the Himalayas a few years ago. Minoo had been part of an Australian expedition climbing Mount Satopanth (23,000 feet) located close to the Gangotri Glacier.

Mrs Mehta, herself a well-known surgeon, was pottering and bustling about the house making sure that the snacks were served hot and everybody got a plateful. The children gaped open-mouthed at the pilots whilst the other members made small talk. Soon, Dr Mehta got everyone quiet and started the formal welcome.

Introducing the pilots, he said, 'These are the brave pilots who were involved in the search and rescue mission of our dear Minoo. They flew for three days at high altitudes, above the limits of the aircraft and searched every nook and cranny of the path to the peak. They flew in bad weather, high turbulence and without adequate oxygen—sometimes landing with a just a few litres of fuel. You would realise that they risked their lives for our dear Minoo and for that, we owe them a standing ovation.'

As he finished, as if orchestrated, all members of the family got up and put their hands together in a rousing felicitation. Dr Mehta, then, handed over some gifts to the pilots as a mark of respect which were accepted most graciously.

***

Many years ago, we had been detailed for a mission to find Minoo Mehta from the high reaches of Mount Satopanth. His father had been at the helipad when the helicopter landed to take on the mission. Wanting to see the terrain for himself, he requested us to take him up a couple of times. We climbed to almost 22,000 feet, way above the limits of the machine. Thankfully, our helicopter could maintain height at this altitude for the search since we had less fuel in our tanks.

After two trips to the place where he was known to have disappeared, the old man was dejected. He told us, 'I think he has gone. There is no reason for you to risk your lives and time any further. Thank you so much for going beyond the call of duty and taking so much pains to search for my son. I do believe, he has attained the death that he always wanted—in the mountains he so loved—closer to the Almighty.

Please do thank all the people who made this mission possible on behalf of our family. If any of you need any help in life, please do not hesitate to call me!' Saying that, the old man got into his car and drove away to the plains to catch a flight to his hometown, Pune.

He was indeed a brave man to say all that even when he was facing such anguish and pain of losing his only son. We decided that we would put in some more sorties to search for the lost son. We returned the next day and repeated the mission. In our hearts of hearts, we knew that there was no chance for the young doctor with the severe cold conditions and the altitude... but we wanted to give it a good try nevertheless.

Minoo's luck had, indeed, run out. His body was found almost a year later when the snow melted and he was given a snow burial as is traditionally given to mountaineers.

The sortie remained marked as a DNCO (Duty Not Carried Out) in our log books. But Dr Mehta remained in our hearts and I managed to keep in touch with him on my numerous trips to Pune. Although much older than me, he was excellent company and there was much to learn from him.

A few years later, I was posted at a forward base in Rajasthan flying combat missions on attack helicopters. Search and rescue weren't in my scheme of things now, as it was a few years earlier.

One day, an airman approached me and told me that he was in a bit of personal grief. His younger brother had a heart condition which required immediate surgery at a good hospital. He did not know anyone in Pune, which was nearest to his home, and had the best medical facilities available. Neither did he have the money to pay for the same, he told me. As he spoke, the image of Dr Mehta and his parting words flashed in my mind.

I told the young man, 'Let me see what can be done. You go to Pune and meet my doctor friend, Dr Mehta. Please take this letter and gift for him.' Along with a small note, I handed the man a small helicopter model to be presented to Dr Mehta as a memento.

The airman proceeded to Pune immediately and I did not get feedback as to what happened, too caught up with my own move to another base. I did, however, often think of checking with Dr Mehta about the case but it just kept getting pushed to the back of my to-do list for some reason or other.

Almost a year later, on one of my sorties, I landed at a forward base for a scheduled night halt. As I got down from the cockpit, the airman who had come to marshal the aircraft, came rushing towards me. As I looked up after removing my helmet, there he was, a few feet away, giving me a sharp and crisp salute–his face beaming with an ear-to-ear smile.

I saw his name on his overalls and recognised the man. 'Oh! So good to see you!' I said slapping him on his shoulders. Looking at the stripes on his shoulders, I went on, 'So now you are a Sergeant, a senior airman! How is everything with you?'

'Sir, I am fine but I must tell you the story of my brother,' he said.

'Go on!' I told him.

'I reached Pune with your letter and gift and met Dr Mehta. He told me to go to my village and get my brother for a check-up immediately. As I got back after two days, there were a few doctors waiting for us. They carried out the necessary checks and opined that my brother would need an operation soon. The open-heart surgery was carried out and my brother was saved!' said the man smiling with tears in his eyes.

'All is well that ends well! You need not thank me. I just requested Dr Mehta and he went out of his way to help. By the way, who paid for the surgery?' I asked the Airman.

'No sir! I offered him some money which I had borrowed from my friends and relatives. But he didn't accept a penny. He said that since we were doing such a great job in keeping our country safe, it was a repayment from their side for our services!'

As I got into bed that night, I thought of the entire episode. What was the reason for us to risk our lives for an unknown mountaineer who had no reason to be alive in those conditions? What was the reason for us to carry out extra missions when there was no reason to do so? What was the reason for me to keep in touch with Dr Mehta? What was the reason for Dr Mehta to help out an airman whom he didn't know? I slept muddled in my mind but was sure that there was a thread which connected all the reasons together.

Little gestures of gratitude, small acts of courage and

kind words of reassurance had the power to save a life. And the rescue mission that began on the snowy peaks of the Himalayas which couldn't save Minoo Mehta had been, in a sense, completed in the saving another life. Maybe every rescue mission does end in a rescue, if you wait long enough. I realised that there was a reason for everything, after all!

Kick That Tyre And Light The Fire...

.... ✣ ....

As the embers are stoked for the evening
Turf is readied for unfettered gurgling
As autumnal breeze enriches the flow
Contours of shadows take a soft glow
As minds sail beyond the reach of voice
Hearts submit to rhythm of their choice
As desolation or seclusion are impermissible
Laughter and food behave as miracles
As the lively lot genially proposes a toast
Spirits in crystals glide down their throats
As affable sessions around the hearth grow
Grounds for lasting alliances they sow

Reheat...
Rolling for takeoff...
My friend and batchmate, Flying Officer MP Anil Kumar, was racing down the runway with the fire from his engine exhaust, or as we call it in Air Force parlance call, 'reheat'.

This was MP's final takeoff. He was flying into the blue yonder and beyond... maybe beyond the heavens too. The man had been tethered to his wheelchair for too long after a horrific accident brought him out of the cockpit when he was flying at 800 kmph to being pushed around at 8 kmph on spoked wheels.

He had become a quadriplegic and was not able to do anything by himself. But undeterred by life's challenges, MP weaved a new life for himself—a life with a lot of meaning and accomplishments. Accomplishments that many of us 'able bodied' persons would only dream of doing even though we had it all.

MP's life has been explored in detail in his biography, *Born to Fly*. I keep wondering what it was that drove MP to do what he did. Or more importantly, what makes people do things out of the ordinary, sometimes, even at the peril of their life?

Maybe the answer is that it is the fire in their belly—a fire which makes us achieve the impossible, a fire difficult to light but once ignited can't be doused easily... sometimes, subsuming the person himself.

As I look back at the thirty-five plus years of exciting IAF flying, through numerous difficult and demanding missions, I can now relate this fire in the belly to all that we did and achieved.

Maybe, it is this fire that keeps us all going.

Zest For Life

········ ✤ ········

Reflecting on life's magnificence
Celebrating it up to the heavens
Painting rainbows of aspirations
Riding clouds of celebrations
Choosing joy over greatest pains
Lighting lamps of abundance
Filling colors of great significance
Always bursting with exuberance
Forever tantalising your imagination
Such is the vivacity of an artistic genius

Leading Aircraftsman (LAC) Mridul Ghosh was posted at a helicopter unit at Sarsawa, near Saharanpur, Uttar Pradesh. On 4 July 2010, he had just returned by train after a well-earned leave from his hometown. Not finding any air force truck to hitch a ride from the station, he decided to hire an auto rickshaw for the fifteen kilometre ride to the air-base.

It was 9 pm, and the highway was dark with little to no traffic. As the auto chugged along, its weak headlights cutting through the darkness, Mridul thought of how much fun he had had with his friends and family during his leave. He was now excited to meet his comrades at the air base after long. Besides the gossip that would ensue after his arrival, the sweets that his mother had sent along would be shared with all his barrack-mates, spreading happiness.

The short journey was not to have a happy ending.

Just a few kilometres from the base, an over-speeding truck dashed against the small three-wheeler from the rear and sent it tumbling into the bushes, into darkness. Mridul suffered no external injury, but his spine was broken at two places. In hospital, the doctors realised the uselessness of the situation. Mridul was rendered a quadriplegic—paralysed below his neck—only a miracle would make him use his limbs again. In a spur of a moment, his life had taken a U-turn. Devastated mentally, Mridul was in despair—looking down a dark tunnel.

Now, thirty-three years young, he has managed to make a meaningful life for himself. I have been his friend and mentor for long and his story needs to be told. But, instead of me narrating it, I would rather have him tell his story.

***

Hi, I am Mridul Ghosh. At the very outset, I want to make it clear that I want no pity or sympathy from anyone, but through my story, I need people to understand that in life nothing is lost till you lose your breath. So, one must live and live well, in hope of good things to come.

I was born in a poor family in the small village of Gruah, West Bengal in the June of 1988. Ours was a joint family where work was distributed amongst all elders. While my Dadaji (grandfather) was the overall boss, my father was a milkman and looked after our cattle. One of his brothers looked after educating children whereas another looked after tilling the land. Despite poor income, thankfully, we didn't have any shortage of food for the family and we grew up to be strong and hardy boys who almost never fell sick.

My primary school was situated near a pond in the village. It had a huge banyan tree under which our classes were conducted. We didn't even have *chappals* (footwear) to wear to school till we reached fifth standard. Life was simple and fun. I remember all the good times we had while growing up as if they had happened yesterday.

My senior school which housed classes from 5th to twelfth was located in lush green surroundings and catered to the schooling requirements of three villages. Playing football—a game that I loved and still yearn for—along with other games that came our way, I took active interest in my studies and my teachers were very happy with me when I finished at the top of my class in the science stream.

Village life was tough and the situation at home tougher. A lot of hard work was being put in by senior family members and I was waiting to get into an occupation as soon as I could to ease their burden.

As soon as I passed my higher secondary, I got myself a job as an apprentice in the Gun and Shell factory near Kolkata. I had barely spent a year there when an opportunity to join our great Indian Air Force presented itself. I was physically fit and good in studies, so, getting recruited as a technical airman wasn't a problem. I passed my training phase with flying colours and was posted to work on helicopters at a unit in Saharanpur.

And then, everything came crashing down due to the accident. I found myself in a wheelchair and had to be looked after by others to do everything that hitherto I could do myself. I was beaten but not out. The doctors and nurses during my rehabilitation at the hospital in Pune were a source of encouragement for me. They made sure that my morale remained high and soon enough, I found myself at the Paraplegic Rehabilitation Centre at Kirkee, Pune with several other inmates like me.

I met Flying Officer MP Anil Kumar, a fighter pilot who had been crippled due to an accident, and he was the one who motivated me to pick up the tattered threads of my life and make a new life for myself. I met with other people, who despite the blows that life had dealt to them, were doing a lot of productive work. I was inspired to do something for myself too.

I happened to meet Mr Manoj Bhingare and Mr Manji Bhai Ramani at the Rehabilitation Centre, who taught me to paint using my mouth. I was artistic as a youngster, and this had to be nurtured and brought to the fore now through a brush held in my mouth.

Learning to paint with my mouth wasn't easy at all. It required a lot of concentration which gave me a headache and my jaws would pain when I held the brush for longer periods of time. Also, sitting in the wheelchair in a cramped position led to more pains and aches. I endured all this and more with the encouragement from my director, Colonel Mukherjee and the inmates of the home. I held on.

The first painting that I produced wasn't too good but I was determined to try again and again. Soon, I was comfortable and started doing my favourite portraits. Painting became a passion for me and all my energy was now directed towards excelling in this artistry.

There's this sense of freedom and positivity I now experience. There's no competition with anyone but myself. And since it keeps me occupied, those are the hours I forget about my tragedy and losses.

***

Mridul is happy and content with his life. He has made sure that his younger brother and sister get the best of education and are well settled in their jobs. In fact, he flew all the way to his hometown to see his sister married off. He teaches mouth painting art to other soldiers like him and also finds the time to teach computer applications at the Queen Mary Technical Institute for disabled soldiers.

Mridul Ghosh has received many awards for his paintings. His work is auctioned by The Association of Mouth and Foot Painting Artists which brings him some extra money. He has also been awarded Mouth and Foot Painting Association (MFPA) India excellence award for 2020.

In the words of Mridul, 'When life throws an axe in your path, cut down all the weeds, sow the seeds of mettle and grow juicy fruits.' When we come across people who display vibrant qualities to fight the adversities of life, it equips us too–to face life in a better manner. Mridul is one who hasn't been cowed down by anything and is a source of inspiration for all.

Look inwards and you will find an artist within you. He resides in everyone, albeit in different forms. It is for you to nurture this artist and create a beautiful world.

Detailed To Kill

.... ✧ ....

My mission beckons
to be ready to kill
Though it isn't
something like
free will
It is a decision I'll not
think twice about
Enemies
of peace
shouldn't have a doubt
I'm a dove polished
with skills of a hawk
I will stick
to my guns
and walk the talk
I continue
to bloom
like lotus in leisure
But as water hemlock
for good measure

I got down from the high cockpit of my armed helicopter. My legs felt like lead. I was barely able to take the weight on my trembling knees. As I removed my chamois leather gloves, I saw that my hands were trembling too. The storm of thoughts passing my mind made thinking impossible.

The firing had had an effect on my nerves. I had fired a weapon a hundred times before but had never felt this way. The closest I had come to this feeling was when as a child, I had fired my air gun at a sparrow and had managed to kill it. I felt awful then and it only felt worse now.

This time was different. There were no sparrows harmed but real people had been fired upon—with an aim to kill—maybe that was what made it worse. I was suffering from the trauma of killing another human being for the first time in my life and the effect sunk in only after the engines of my helicopter had gone silent.

Downing a few glasses of cold water and ordering a coffee for myself, I walked into the crew room like a zombie, still shaking from head to toe, my mind numb. I sank into the cushions of the couch and tried to come to grips with the situation.

We were part of the United Nations Peace Keeping Force in the Democratic Republic of Congo or DRC.

Our duty entailed maintaining peace by the 'use of force.'

The action had taken place near Goma where we lived on the eastern flank of the DRC. The weather was salubrious and the place so beautiful. But there was tension and strife in this politically weak and war-torn country where no one knew whose side the other was on.

Ironically, Chinese, Pakistanis and Indians—sworn enemies back at home, worked shoulder to shoulder to maintain peace in this foreign land—a mission that hadn't met success for many years.

The DRC had once been a rich country and the Congolese currency had been even stronger than the US dollar. It was still rich but the riches were now being siphoned off by illegal exploitation, many a neighboring nation's economy gaining from the spoils. This was a nation locked in the middle of the Dark Continent. There seemed to be no hope. The Congolese Army was made up of underpaid and undertrained militia who brandished their weapons to rape, loot and kill poor locals who could barely feed themselves. Not much could be done to stop this till we established some sort of order and stability in the region.

Within this army were dissident groups, who would often break away from the so called 'regulars' and the fighting for supremacy would begin. Often, we, the UN troops, would get caught in the melee and crossfire. Some of our peacekeepers had even been killed.

It was 2006-07. We had heard of a big faction of the army led by one self-styled 'General' Laurent Nkunda commencing fighting near the town of Sake. Sake was located at the base of the hills and was close to our town of Goma. As per intelligence inputs and our reading of the battle, we had visualised that the fighting would peter out near Sake and the militia would go back into hiding in a few days as had happened earlier.

But in life, and especially in war, things don't generally happen as we think they will. One night as we slept, we were woken up by gunfire. It appeared that the militia were, indeed, closing in on Goma. If they managed to take over the town, they would get us too, and destroy the entire establishment that had been painstakingly set up over time.

We got information from the locals that as many as 10,000 militias were advancing towards Goma. If the militants found their way into town, we would be looking at many casualties and Congo would lose an important town.

The warring faction had to be stopped and stopped short of Goma, no matter what the cost.

Meetings and briefings went on through the night as the fighting was heard coming closer and closer. We accelerated efforts to get the 'go ahead' to use our weapons in self defence. Our action to stop the 'enemy' had to be quick and swift and it was planned that way.

The army was requested to send out troops in their four Armed Personal Carriers (APCs) to block the advance of the militia just outside the town. With the extended reach of our helicopters, we were to try and stop them before they came within the killing distance of these APCs.

We were all set—the aircrafts loaded with rockets and guns, waiting a go ahead from the UN HQs at New York. We got it soon enough and it now dawned on us that that we had been drawn into a war in a foreign country—fighting against an enemy who really wasn't our enemy.

The first planned mission was to Sake in the late evening hours. We were to fly towards the town and take stock of the situation from above. Maybe seeing us flying around would force them to disengage. But things had gotten out of hand. Our flight overhead the area did not have any effect.

In the captain's seat, flying with me was a young pilot. We reached the area and spotted a pick-up kind of jeep with about 8 to 10 militia armed with guns speeding away on the road towards the hills. While I focused my sights on to them, I transmitted to the commander on ground, 'Request identity of people travelling in camouflage pick up jeep heading out of Sake towards the south.'

Pat came the reply on radio. 'Roger sir, stand by….' and after a few seconds his voice crackled again, 'That is the local commander of the militia with his men and he seems to be heading towards the hills to regroup!'

'Kill them sir!' he pleaded after a pause.

'Roger, Over and Out!'

As we went closer to the jeep which seemed to be traveling at breakneck speed billowing plumes of dust on the dirt road, we were spotted. This forced them into hiding in the foliage. The cat and mouse game had begun.

We orbited a distance away with my sight fixed on to the road where we had lost them. When they thought we had lost them, the jeep appeared into the open and onto the road. We tried to get a shot at them. As we neared for the kill, they repeated the maneuver of disappearing into the thicket. These guys were good at evasive maneuvering!

The chase was getting exasperating now and tension was building in the cockpit. We had about 10 to 15 minutes of fuel left to get them otherwise the mission would be a failure. Darkness, which was fast approaching, would turn the tables in their favour.

With all the modern gadgetry, it was simple to keep track of the road. And I did exactly that—peering through my gunsight. But we needed to get physically close to them, stabilise our flight and put our 'pipper' on them—and that required at least a couple of minutes of exposure time.

It was decided that we move further away from the area and duck down to very low heights over a grassy piece of land. I realised that if we allowed them to climb a small hillock—a hillock very close to their hiding area, we would have our job cut out. I briefed the crew of my plan and pumped them up.

'Let us have some good shooting today! Recheck all switches on!'

It was a moment of reckoning for us in the cockpit. We had to deliver the weapons on target.

As predicted, the jeep came out of its hiding and commenced its climb up the hillock. It would soon be travelling 90 degrees to us and could be clearly seen against the high ground. We zoomed up to 700 feet and commenced a shallow dive towards the target.

'Three kilometres Check rocket master on and switches selected to salvo,' I started the count down.

'2.5... Confirm sight selections to automatic?'

'2 km... Steady, steady... hold her steady!'

'1.5... Ready to fire... Standby...'

'1.4...'

'1.3...'

'3-2-1... FIRE!'

The aircraft seemed to stop in mid-air as rocket after rocket left the pods whooshing away on their final journey in a stream of smoke. The target did not stand a chance with a volley of sixteen projectiles. I looked for impact through my sight. Amidst a cloud of smoke and dust, the rockets seemed to have straddled the target. We heard the explosions one after the other and saw the bright flashes of light as they impacted around the vehicle.

We decided to do another run-in to carry out damage assessment. This time we had to be ready to fire another salvo, if required.

The smoke and dust of the impacting rockets had cleared as we came in for the second pass. Through my sight, I saw that the jeep had been reduced to a mass of contorted steel. I could see that the driver was dead in his seat while the others had jumped off and died due to the flying shrapnel. There seemed to be no survivors.

We flew back to base relieved that we had got the target. It would soon be time for the next mission.

We practically did not get any sleep over the next three days that the fighting continued and when it eventually stopped, we were on the verge of collapse. It was black coffee and the josh of the men on the ground that made us go on. And yes, there was our squadron doctor too, who kept a watchful eye on us through those days.

With the local militia leaders killed, the fight had lost its momentum and General Nkunda ordered his men back into the hills to regroup to fight another day.

When the guns fell silent, bodies of the men killed in battle started arriving for burial at the graveyard located right next to our camp at Goma. We saw truckloads of them. Some of them, of course, had been killed by our action. It was a sad sight, and my stomach still churns when I remember the episode.

While flying and firing from the air, it is easy to pull the trigger from a standoff distance. The soldier on ground has to fight and kill the enemy from close range and sometimes even in hand-to-hand combat. My admiration for the soldier on the ground went up a notch. What nerves of steel he must have to kill the enemy at close range!

Waves That Changed Lives

········ ✣ ········

The cycles of
Vapors to oceans
Pebbles to mountains
Carbon to diamonds
Validate the worth of transformation

The changes in
Leaves on the branches of trees
Summers and winter breeze
Soft skin wrinkling with aging
Validate the permanence of transience

Wave after wave kept lashing the tiny island which had borne the brunt of a severe earthquake.

It was early morning hours of 26 December 2004, and unlike how James Bond likes his cocktail, the residents of this tiny island were both shaken and stirred in a cauldron of salty water.

One and a half kilometres in length and fifty to sixty feet high, these waves rose from the depth of the ocean, travelling at seventy plus kilometres per hour, ravaging whatever came their way. There were seven of them and whatever one wave couldn't finish, the others did.

In a matter of forty-five minutes, after the 9.0 magnitude earthquake and the tsunami had hit everything had changed. The residents of the Air Force Station at Car Nicobar, who had enjoyed a late-night Christmas party on 25 December and were longing to chill on the Sunday morning of the 26 December were battered, bruised and broken—figuratively and literally. They looked for their belongings and missing ones, —who, in all probability had been taken away by the churning waters of the ocean.

There was mayhem everywhere one looked. Dead humans and cattle lay in the concrete rubble that were once homes. Trees lay uprooted and the entire island was strewn with smashed cars and trucks and household stuff

—clothes, toys, gas cylinders, furniture, and even cash, ornaments and more.

Wailing and sobbing parents clutched the dead bodies of their young ones to their bosoms and looked to the sky for mercy. Others looked around and under the rubble to see if they could find some life there. Luckier ones who had just lost their homes went about scavenging for cash, valuables and belongings kept inside their now broken households, looking for anything that could be retrieved.

Everyone, very much, were on their own, trying to survive and make the best of whatever they could. It was a heart wrenching scene.

With no power, no drinking water, food and no communication with the outside world, hope too seemed to have vanished. How could everything change in a moment? What wrong had they done to deserve this? Were they atoning for their sins of the present or past life?

Many questions but no answers.

In a while, the panic subsided to a level where logical thinking and reasoning was possible. But the earth continued to rumble, the ocean churned the belongings it had collected from the land in a whirlpool of brown water and the survivors on land still wailed and sobbed uncontrollably. For those who left for the heavens, life had ended, but for those who stayed alive, everything that 'life' meant for them, changed. Very soon, all the affected residents were moved out of the Island to Mainland India, 1500 km away to begin anew. A new life, scarred permanently by what they had gone through.

A team of seventy men of the IAF were sent from the Mainland to start rebuilding the Islands to its former pristine glory—a task as tall and large as the waves that had destroyed it. Taken out of the comfort of their homes and family life, the lives of these seventy men were also set to change. They didn't have even a faint idea of what a tsunami was and what it could do till they reached the islands and saw it for themselves.

Rescue, relief and rehabilitation followed the aftermath of the devastation. The experience remains etched on the mind of every soldier of every hue who took part in these operations.

Learning to live minimalistic, to take things as they come, the art of managing men and material, the art of improvisation (*jugaad*), to work as a team, to be kind, compassionate and focused at the same time... so much and more was learnt in these changed surroundings so alien to the men who were tasked to restore normalcy.

Difficulties notwithstanding, it was the logistics chain management which was most problematic due to the remoteness of the island. Like war, all plans went out of the window since the scene changed as you blinked. In this SFCS (Super Fast Changing Scenario), no plans could really work since goalposts kept moving.

It was exasperating, tiresome and a difficult time. But this did not deter the men on guard. A promise had been given to the Chief. The base had to stand on its feet again in 100 days. The challenge had to be met come rain, hail or snow or whatever nature had to offer. Day after day, night after night, the seventy men pushed on like good soldiers, and nothing wore them down till some semblance of order was established.

Despite the negativity of the devastation, the experience of working on the Island was wholesome. It had its moments of grief and sorrow, of happiness and joy, of death and destruction. And it changed the way these men looked at life. It made them resilient, mentally tough, instilled in them a positive attitude and a will to win. It taught them that even if life turned cruel, it still had something positive to offer if you looked hard enough for it.

The change that the tsunami brought into people's life was set in stone, never to be forgotten.

I know this story because I was right there, leading my men through thick and thin.

PS: Many years later, I wrote about our experiences of the tsunami in my first book, *A Few Good Men and the Angry Sea*.

Other Books By The Author

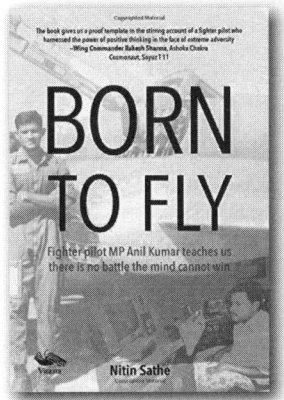